Role of Pakistan in India's Energy security

An Issue Brief

Role of Pakistan in India's Energy security

by

**Major General (Retired) Ajay Kumar Chaturvedi,
AVSM, VSM**

Centre for Joint Warfare Studies (CENJOWS)

New Delhi

Vij Books India Pvt Ltd

New Delhi (India)

Published by

Vij Books India Pvt Ltd

(Publishers, Distributors & Importers)
2/19, Ansari Road, Darya Ganj
New Delhi - 110002
Phones: 91-11-43596460, 91-11- 47340674
Fax: 91-11-47340674
e-mail : vijbooks@rediffmail.com
web: www.vijbooks.com

ISBN: 978-93-82652-18-2

Index

List of Figures and Tables

Figures-

Tables

Abstract

India is short of energy despite one of the lowest per capita energy consumption. It is indeed of interest that most of the forms of energy which are part of the present Energy Matrix of India, suffer from some problem or the other. These are either due to quality of resource (coal), shortage of resource (Natural Uranium, Petroleum based resources), lack of technologies for indigenous resources (Thorium, renewable sources), shortage of adequate infrastructure for their exploitation (entire country not yet connected by power grid, internal network of pipelines). Next major issue is that the gestation period for the growth of most of the desired technologies to exploit local resources is quite long and as such there is a need to go for exploitation of resources which are either readily available or can be exploited by resorting to import of energy resources. This is where Natural Gas assumes importance and has potential for exploitation in short to medium term. In this connection import from West Asia and Central Asia holds good promise. Pakistan has a very pivotal position in the import of natural gas from either of the two sources. Involving Pakistan while may be froth with danger due to volatile situation in that country or an persisting anti Indian sentiments existing there, but another way to look at it would be that such a relationship may give boost to Pakistan's economy and enhance interdependence between the two countries leading to improvement in the relations. This paper attempts to examine all these related issues.

Foreword

Energy is one of the main drivers for the growth of a country which entails among other things economic growth. The sustained economic strength is one of the most important elements of the demonstrated Comprehensive National Power (CNP) of a nation. It is therefore essential that a nation which wishes to enhance its CNP makes a concerted effort to ensure provision of energy for all its activities related to growth and also to meet the needs of its citizens. Energy Security of the nation is the measure of the sustained availability of energy to link demand and supply equation in such a way that the outcome is not negative.

India is although endowed with enough energy bearing resources but presently its energy availability to meet its growing demand without import is not feasible. This gap between potential and reality needs to be bridged. While a long term solution needs to be worked out by the planners to exploit indigenous resources, a simultaneous effort to ensure sustained availability of energy in the form for which technologies are indigenously available needs to be pursued in short and medium term. Import, in such a contingency, is the answer, particularly of those resources for which technologies for exploitation are readily available. Oil and natural gas are those desired resources. Due to certain geo-political developments and technological innovations the natural gas is becoming an attractive option. But abundant natural gas from land route is available either in Iran or Central Asia. Transportation of gas from either region entails its travel through Pakistan. Therefore, it becomes essential to examine the viability of such an option. However, arriving at the decision to transport gas through Pakistan and thereafter build infrastructure will have certain gestation period therefore what could be the solution for the interim. Recent technological breakthrough by the US in the field of Shale Gas has thrown up new options for India in the field of Liquefied Natural Gas (LNG) imports. Can India exploit this new geo-economic development?

To examine all these issues, the CENJOWS had tasked Maj Gen

(Retd) AK Chaturvedi, AVSM, and VSM. The present Issue Brief is an outcome of his research. The author has attempted to look at the issue in entirety and hopefully his research will be able to assist the decision makers to coalesce their thought.

CENJOWS
HQ IDS, New Delhi
25 May 2013

(KB Kapoor)
Maj Gen (Retd)
Executive Director

Acknowledgement

I am thankful to the hierarchy of the CENJOWS, particularly Maj Gen (Retd) KB Kapoor, VSM, the Executive Director, CENJOWS for reposing faith in my capability to address the issues which he wanted to be examined *de-novo*.

There is a lot of work which a number of scholars have already done on related subjects and I have had the honour to quote them in my research. I am thankful to each one of them and have given them due credit in my research.

My sincere thanks to Shri BK Chaturvedi, Member (Energy) Planning Commission, Shri Vivek Rae, Secretary Ministry of Petroleum & Natural Gas, Shri Prabhat Kumar, Joint Secretary, Energy Security & Investment & Technology Promotion, Ministry of External Affairs, Shri DK Sarraf, Managing Director & CEO, ONGC VIDESH LTD, Dr Shebonti Ray Dadhwal, Research Fellow, Institute for Defence Studies and Analyses, New Delhi for their very useful inputs and helping me to steer the research in the right direction.

I also would like to place on record my thanks to Brig (Dr) PS Siwach, my guide for the Ph D programme (India's Energy Security: 2030) at Manipal University Jaipur for his useful suggestions and help he rendered to me to clear my mind on many attended management issues.

In the end, my sincere gratitude to those, who supported me from behind the scenes. First in that list is Col AK Singh, Secretary CENJOWS, a friend of many years, who has always been a friend, philosopher and guide to me and this occasion, was no exception and Second, my wife Mrs Renu Chaturvedi, who, like always, has been a pillar of strength to me.

Lucknow
25 May 2013

(AK Chaturvedi)
Maj Gen (Retd)

Abbreviations

Word/ Phrase	Abbreviation
Barrel	Bbl
Billion Cubic Feed	BCF
Billion Cubic Metres	BCM
Central Asian Republics (Kazakhstan, Uzbekistan, Turkmenistan, Tajikistan and Kyrgyzstan)	CAR
Central Intelligence Agency	CIA
Coal India Limited	CIL
Cubic Meters	CUM
Capacity Utilisation Factor	CUF
Coal Bed Methane	CBM
Compressed Natural Gas	CNG
Compound Annual Growth Rate	CAGR
Directorate of Hydrocarbons	DGH
Energy Information Administration	EIA
Exploration and Production	E&P
Federally Administered Tribal Area	FATA
Frontier Region	FR
Free Trade Agreement	FTA
Gas Authority of India Limited	GAIL
Government of India	GOI
Gross domestic Product	GDP

International Energy Agency	IEA
Integrated Gasification Combined Cycle	IGCC
Iran-Pakistan-India	IPI
Japanese custom Cleared Crude Prices	JCCC
Kilo Calories	Kcal
Kilograms of Oil Equivalent	KgOE
Kilo Watt Hour	KWH
Krishna Godavari	KG
Liquefied Natural Gas	LNG
Liquefied Petroleum Gas	LPG
Mega watt	MW
Memorandum of Understanding	MoU
Metres Below Sea Floor	Mbsf
Million Metric Standard Cubic Metres Per Day	MMSCMD
Million Metric Tonnes	MMT
Million Tons of Oil Equivalent	MTOE
Million Metric Tonnes Per Annum	MMTPA/ MTPA
Million British Thermal Unit	MBTU/ MMBTU
Ministry of External Affairs	MEA
Ministry of Petroleum and Natural gas	MoP&NG
Multi Organisation Team	MOT
National Energy Fund	NEF
National gas Hydrate Programme	NGHP
Natural Gas	NG

New Exploration Licensing Policy	NELP
New Policies Scenario	NPS
North Eastern Region	NER
Oil and Natural Gas Corporation	ONGC
ONGC Videsh Limited	OVL
Oil India Limited	OIL
People's Republic of China	PRC
Petroleum Planning and Analysis Cell	PPAC
Production Sharing Agreement	PSA
Production Sharing Contract	PSC
Reliance Gas Transportation Infrastructure Limited	RGTIL
Research & Development	R&D
Russian Federation	Russia
Tonnes of Oil Equivalent	TOE
Total Primary Energy Demand	TPED
Trillion Cubic Feet	TCF
Trillion Cubic Meters	TCM
Turkmenistan-Afghanistan-Pakistan-India	TAPI
United States of America	USA
United States of America Department of Energy	USDOE
United States Geological Survey	USGS
World Economic Organisation	WEO

Role of Pakistan in India's Energy Security

Section-1: Background

Introduction

Energy is vital for the economic growth of any nation. In this connection it needs to be appreciated that the energy is a vital input into production and therefore higher growth rate is feasible, only if sufficient energy is available to sustain the industrial production. The issue has a further knot and that is; its availability at a competitive price to make it economically viable. Therefore for a sustained economic growth availability of reliable energy at optimum economic rate is a prerequisite. This, in nutshell, is the essence of the Energy Security. Thus it can easily be concluded that the Energy security is the measure of the economic strength of a nation and also by implication a measure of the CNP.

Conceptual Framework - Energy Security is an important input among other inputs to 'Comprehensive national power' with linkages among various elements to the Comprehensive national power and also with the other external influencing factors. A conceptual framework outlining the various linkages in understanding the impact of the energy security on the comprehensive national power is as depicted in the Figure-1.1.

Figure-1.1

Conceptual Framework

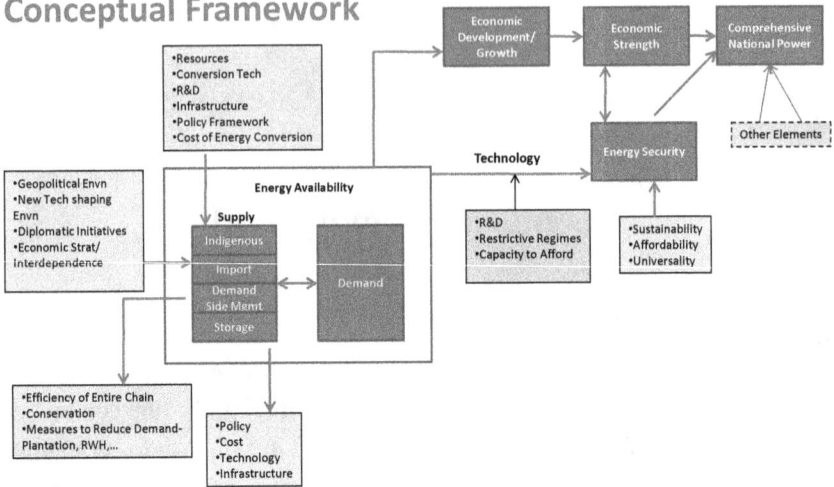

India is the fourth largest consumer of energy in the world after the United States of America (USA), People's Republic of China (PRC) and Russian Federation (Russia). However her energy resources are quite limited; especially for technologies which are in vogue. Therefore for a sustained economic development necessary for the growth of the country on the world power ladder, there is a need to optimise use of all available indigenous resources and supplement them with imports in such a way that the resultant relationship with the concerned countries is based on interdependence to reduce the Nation's strategic vulnerability, give a boost to research and development of technologies for the energy bearing resources available in abundance within the country, enhance energy intensity, conserve energy as much as possible and finally evolve systems and procedures to co-ordinate conversion of energy bearing resources into power and its conveyance to desired destination within the envelope of minimum environmental degradation and affordable cost.

Overview of Energy

The total primary energy supply (both commercial and non-commercial) increased from 89.6x106 TOE (tonnes of oil equivalent) in 1953-54 to about 365x106 TOE in 1996-97. The share of non-commercial fuels has declined from 72 percent in 1953-54 to about 32 percent in 1996-97. Fuel wood accounts for nearly 65 percent of the total non-commercial energy consumed in the country. Of the indigenous primary commercial energy production, the relative share of oil and natural gas has increased from 1.2 percent in 1950-51 to 27.9 percent in 1996-97 (as compared to nearly 34 percent in 1989-90). The share of coal which was 98 percent in 1950-51 has declined to 67.7 percent in 1996-97. The changes in the pattern of primary energy supplies are shown in Table- 1.1.

Table -1.1

Trends in Supply of Primary Commercial Energy

Domestic production (in MTOE)	2000–01 (Actual)	2006–07 (Actual)	2011–12 (Provisional)	2016–17 (Projected)	2021–22 (Projected) (%growth on 2000-01 figures)
Coal	130.61	177.24	222.16	308.55	400 (206%)
Lignite	6.43	8.76	10.64	16.80	29 (351%)
Crude Oil	33.40	33.99	39.23	42.75	43 (28.7%)
Natural Gas	25.07	27.71	42.79	76.13	103 (310.8%)
Hydro Power	6.40	9.78	11.22	12.90	17 (165.6%)
Nuclear Power	4.41	4.91	8.43	16.97	30 (580%)
Renewable Energy	0.13	0.87	5.25	10.74	20 (15284.6%)
Total Domestic commercial Energy	206.45	263.28	339.72	481.84	642.00 (211%)
Non-commer-cial Energy	1 136.64	153.28 (1.93)	174.20 (2.6 %)	187.66 (1.5 %)	202.16 (1.5 %)
Total	343.09	416.56	513.92	669.50	844.16 (146%)
IMPORTS					
Coal	11.76	24.92	54.00	90.00	150.00 (1175.5%)
Petroleum Products	77.25	98.41	129.86	152.44	194.00 (151.1)
LNG		0 8.45	12.56	24.80	31.00 (310%)

Hydro power	0	0.26	0.45	0.52	0.60 (60%)
Total Net Imports	**89.01**	**132.04**	**196.87**	**267.76**	**375.609 (322%)**
Total Commercial Energy (growth over the previous five years)	295.46	396.32 (5.01 %)	536.59 (6.25 %)	749.60 (6.91 %)	1017.60 (6.30 %)
Total Primary Energy	**432.01**	**549.60 (4.09 %)**	**710.79 (5.28 %)**	**937.26 (5.69 %)**	**1219.76 (5.41 %)**

*MTOE: Million Tons of Oil Equivalent.

Source: Planning Commission.

Note: Figures in brackets are annual average growth rates over the previous five years' period

Observations:

- There is massive growth in the production of all types of energy sources except oil which has more or less remained stagnant.

- Growth in case of Nuclear and Renewable Sources may be statistically significant but as the datum at the start was quite low the growth cannot be considered realistic except that these sources are highly important and are likely to help India achieve energy self sufficiency in due course of time but a little more analysis is needed to ascertain as to how long will it take.

- Relevance of Natural Gas also gets highlighted substantially.

- If domestic production is increasing so is the import which is likely to grow by 322 percent.

- LNG which is considered a kind of replacement (more appropriately supplement) for oil will also be imported in large quantities. Therefore for better management of this vital resource the planners will have to start the process of enhancing its input into the energy matrix by all sources; import, acquisition of gas equities abroad, accelerating indigenous exploration and evolving measures to control demand through better demand side management.

Energy Efficiency-

Table-1.2

Energy Intensity of Selected Representative Countries for the Year 2010

Country	Energy Intensity* (KgOE/US $)
United Kingdom	0.102
Germany	0.121
Japan	0.125
Brazil	0.134
United States of America	0.173
PRC	0.283
Republic of Korea	0.189
India	0.191

* Energy Intensity indicates energy required to produce one unit of GDP in Purchasing Power Parity terms.

Source: Plan Document of 12th Five Year Plan.

Assessment: As can be seen from Table-1.2 above, as compared to other developed/ emerging countries, except China the utilisation of energy in India is not as efficient as it should have been. Though the Energy Intensity has declined from 1.09 in 1981 to 0.62 in 2011 but still a long way is to be traversed. The inefficiency of utilisation of the meagre resources accentuates the energy deficiency further.

Demand versus Production- Domestic production of energy resources is projected to increase, however import dependence will continue at a high level. Crude oil (more than 78 percent) and coal, LNG and crude oil taken together (36 percent) in the terminal year of the Twelfth Plan is the projection. (Sec: 14.14, 12th Plan Document). The share of natural gas and liquefied natural gas (LNG) is projected to rise from 8.5 percent to 13 percent in the same period. The combined share of oil and natural gas in energy consumption was 24.7 percent in 2011–12 and is expected to be about the same in 2021–22. (Sec: 14.12, 12th Plan Document). It needs to be appreciated that Oil imports during 2010-11 cost the nation $100 billion which is 26 percent higher than last year and as such is a cause of alarm because it contributes substantially to the fiscal deficit of the country. (Energy security hand Book).

Sectoral Energy Demand-   Sectoral energy demand reflects the economic structure of a country. In 1990, the building sector was India's largest energy consumer, representing 42 percent of India's total primary energy demand (TPED), using biomass as the major fuel. The share of buildings dropped to 29 percent in 2009 and will decrease to about 18 percent in 2035. The industry sector consumed approximately 22 percent of TPED in 1990 and will remain similar until 2035. The power sector has been the primary force behind energy demand growth in India. Its share expanded from 23 percent to 38 percent of TPED from 1990 to 2009. This was attributable to soaring demand for electricity for industry uses and residential/commercial activities. With this trend, the share of the power sector will continue growing to almost 42 percent in 2035 under New Policies Scenario (NPS)-450 of worked out by the World Economic Organisation (WEO) in 2011. The transport sector represented 8 percent of energy in 1990 and will reach 14 percent in 2035 under NPS-450, a small but significant growth, as 90 percent of transport energy consumption will be based on oil.

Figure- 1.2

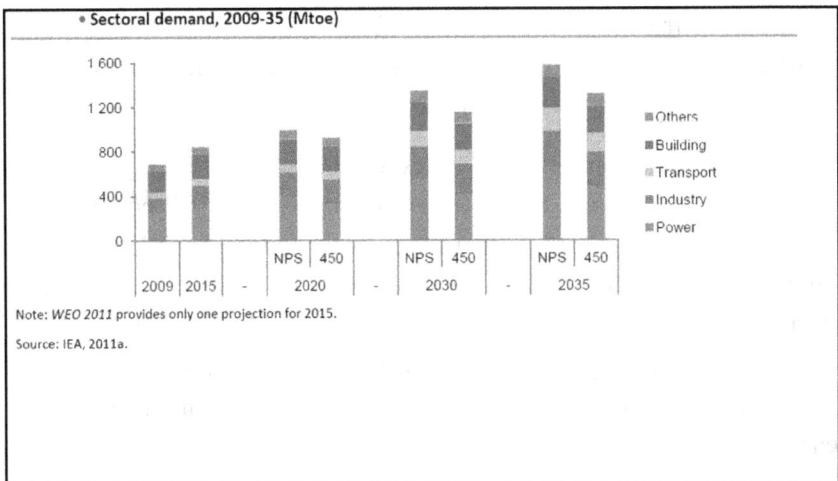

Note: *WEO 2011 provides only one projection for 2015.*

Source: IEA, 2011a.

Domestic Energy Production- has grown in India from 291 MTOE in 1990 to 502 MTOE in 2009 at a Compound Annual Growth Rate (CAGR) of 2.9 percent. Considering India's demand growth at a CAGR of 4 percent for the same duration, domestic supply could not keep up with the demand. Biomass was the largest production source with 46 percent share in 1990, but dropped to 33 percent in 2009. The largest production volume addition came from coal production, which increased from 104 MTOE in 1990 to 244 MTOE in 2009 at a CAGR 4.6 percent. Coal also represented almost half of total domestic energy production. The fastest growing fuel is, however, natural gas, which increased domestic energy production to 38 MTOE in 2009 from 10 MTOE in 1990 at a CAGR of 7.0 percent. On the other hand, crude oil production growth remained at CAGR 0.5 percent for the same period, whilst crude demand increased by 5.1 percent.

Figure-1.3

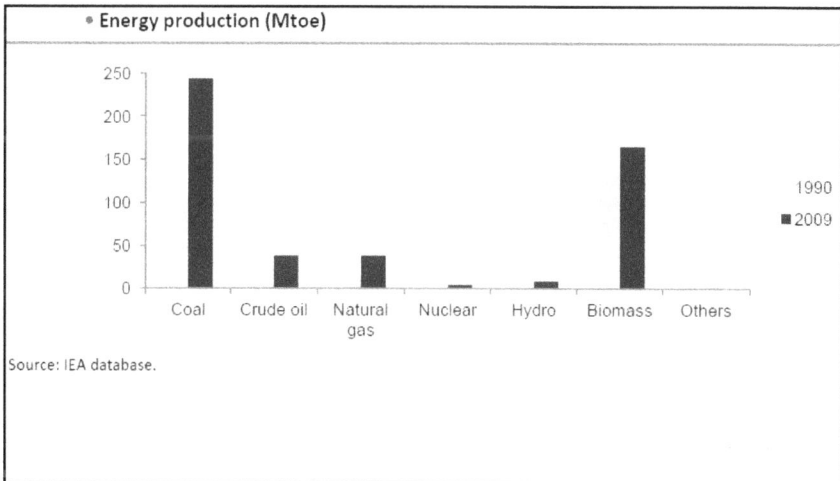

Source: IEA database.

Table- 1.3

Share of Each Fuel in Total Energy Production And Consumption (In Percentage)

	2000–01 Actual	2006–07 Actual	2011–12 (Provi-sional)	2016–17 (Project-ed)	2021–22 (Pro-jected)
Share in Commercial Energy Production					
Coal and Lignite	66.38	70.65	68.53	67.52	66.82
Crude Oil	16.18	12.91	11.55	8.87	6.70
Natural Gas	12.14	10.52	1260	15.80	16.04
Hydro Power	3.10	3.71	3.30	2.68	2.65
Nuclear Power	2.14	1.86	2.48	3.52	4.67
Renewable Energy	0.06	0.33	1.55	2.23	3.12
Share in Total Commercial Energy Supply					
Coal and Lignite	50.36	53.22	53.45	55.41	56.90
Crude Oil	37.45	33.41	31.51	26.04	23.29
Natural Gas	8.49	6.99	10.32	13.46	13.17
Hydro Power	2.17	2.53	2.17	1.79	1.73
Nuclear Power	1.49	1.24	1.57	2.26	2.95
Renewable Energy	0.04	0.22	0.98	1.43	1.97

Source: Planning Commission (12th Plan Document)

Observation:

• It can be concluded that while contribution of oil and hydro will reduce, the share of coal natural gas, nuclear and renewable will increase.

- Due to versatility and industry equipping pattern natural gas becomes in short to medium term reasonably important

Import Dependence- As the growth in energy demand outpaced domestic energy production, India's dependence on imported energy intensified. From 1990 to 2009, as total energy imports increased from 34 MTOE to 236 MTOE, India's import dependence increased from 11 percent to 35 percent. The largest source of import increase was crude oil, representing 70 percent of the total increase. India imported only 21 MTOE of crude oil in 1990, but its dependence on foreign crude oil was already high at 61 percent. The Total volume of imported crude, reached 162 MTOE or 81 percent of India's crude demand, in 2009. Natural gas imports were zero in 1990 and increased to 10 MTOE or 21 percent of total natural gas demand in 2009 (IEA Statistics). It is noteworthy that presently India only imports LNG and not piped gas. As such, the availability and affordability of imported energy has become a key factor in determining India's energy demand growth.

Figure-1.4

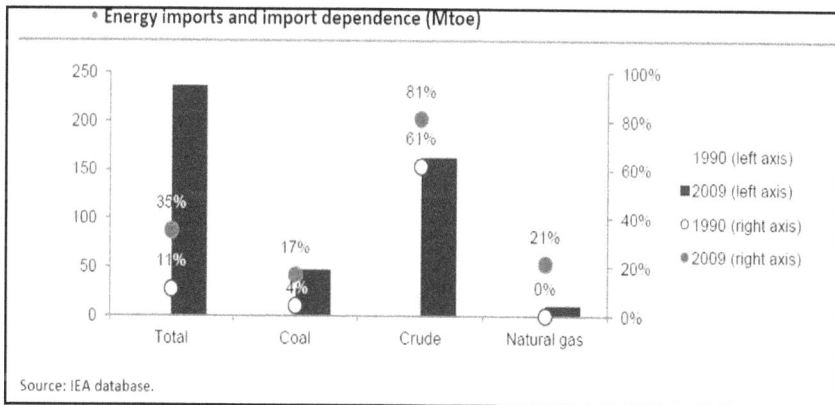

Above figure clearly brings out that coal import is on the increase basically as the local coal is neither very good in quality (high ash content) nor is efficient (lower calorific value as compared to imported coal. Similarly natural gas import is increasing and because of various reasons has been accepted as the preferred energy resource. Importance of the natural gas will be discussed in the next section. Import of crude has already reached a point (81 percent) where dependence on imported crude will be bad for economy due to spiralling price of crude in the international market (Sun-Joo Ahn and Dagmar Graczyk).

Relevance of Natural Gas

To appreciate the importance of Natural gas and Oil it would be logical to analyse the status of other sources with respect to their availability and ease of their technical exploitation. The important sources are discussed in following paragraphs.

Coal- currently provides 60 percent of India's commercial energy consumption. Between 1984 and 2004, coal consumption in India increased from 140 million metric tons (MMT) to over 400 MMT annually, growing at a rate of 5.4 percent per year. Of the coal consumed, 90 percent is produced domestically while about 10 percent is imported, primarily from Australia and South Africa. (A Report of the Planning Commission of India). India is forced to import coal because the high ash content and low calorific value of domestic supplies make it inadequate for certain purposes. Thus, over 70 percent of domestic coal production is used in thermal power generation. Indian coal averages about 4100 kcal/kg compared to imported coal, which has calorific values of about 6000 kcal/kg. The poor quality of Indian coal has led to an acute shortage of higher quality coking coal. Since the quality of India's coal has actually been deteriorating over the past few decades, India has had to rely on ever-larger supplies of imported coal. Contrary to conventional logic, imported coal is not significantly cheaper than imported oil or gas. As a competitive fuel source, the prices of coal imports rise and fall with prices of crude. Thus, a coal dependent power sector does not protect India from sudden price hikes, although such increases would admittedly be less dramatic in the coal industry. Coal imports also require development of a very costly infrastructure. (David Temple).

Nuclear- India is currently dependent on uranium to fuel its nuclear reactors which is adequate to support, at best, a 10,000 MW power generation programme. India, however, possesses roughly one quarter of the world's thorium, a material used in the uranium enrichment process. (BBC News) In view of this limitation of the resource, it aims to eventually develop the technology to use thorium and uranium-233, a by-product of the uranium enrichment process, for nuclear power. However it needs to be noted that this course of action is based on an assumption that thorium-based fast-breeder reactors would be developed at the earliest, which would allow India to graduate to Stage III of India's Nuclear Programme. It is anticipated that with this strategy India is likely to have a self-sustaining nuclear programme that would meet the core of its energy needs. As of yet, this technology is far from being operational; of the three stages necessary to implement the strategy, only the first has been completed. Roughly, the process consists of creating Pressurized Heavy Water Reactors (stage 1), Fast Breeder Reactors (stage 2), and reactors to process uranium-233 and thorium-232 (stage 3). Although the Pressurized Heavy Water Reactors have been created, the process took far longer than anticipated, and even optimistic projections foresee the next two stages requiring at least another thirty-five years. Thus the realist picture that emerges is that even by the most optimistic projections India is likely to create a capacity to produce only 16 percent of its electricity from nuclear power by 2052.   Thus, although nuclear power may provide India with a long term option, it is unlikely to serve a defining role in the next half a century.

Hydro-Power & Renewable Energy- Until 1980, the growth rate of hydro and thermal power generation in India was roughly equal. Even presently, power generation based on hydro-generation plays a decent role in India's electricity generation, providing 30,936 MW of electricity per year, or 26 percent of the total electricity production. (An Official communiqué of the Ministry of Power, Government of India (GOI)). It is estimated that even if India were to exploit its full hydro potential of 150,000 MW, the contribution of hydro energy to the energy mix will only be around 1.9-2.2 percent by 2032. (Planning Commission, GOI, n-1). Solar Energy is another form of renewable energy which has good potential for growth in India. However, presently cost is the biggest constraint (Rs. 20/KWH). It is anticipated that if the present trend of the growth is maintained it has a potential to generate approximately 1,200 MTOE of power by 2032. (Planning Commission, GOI, n-1). Other forms of renewable sources at the moment are either not commercially viable or are too insignificant and at best can be considered suitable for local use at the present state of their development.

Wind Energy- Although the current contribution of the Wind power to the grid is only about 3,000 MW, but India's wind energy potential is assessed to be around 65,000 MW by the Wind Power Society of India. The wind energy currently contributes less than 1 MTOE of power to India each year. Even if India harnesses all of its wind potential, the total contribution of wind energy to India's energy mix is unlikely to exceed 10 MTOE at best. (Planning commission, n-1).

Oil- The country is not self-sufficient in oil and oil products. As a result, the import dependence of the country for oil has been increasing over the time. The degree of self-sufficiency in oil which was around 35 percent in 1975 (Bombay High got operationalised in 1974), increased up to 1984-85 and was the highest at 70 percent during that year. It has started declining thereafter in the wake of the decline in the indigenous production of the crude oil and rising demand for the petroleum products. The annual average growth rate of the total energy requirement is expected to accelerate from 5.1 per cent per year in the Eleventh Plan to 5.7 per cent per year in the Twelfth Plan and 5.4 per cent per year in the Thirteenth Plan. The faster growth in supply in the Twelfth Plan is in part a reflection of the need to meet suppressed demand (Sec 14.10 of the 12th Plan Document).

Table-1.4

Import Dependence of Oil

Year	Quantity in Million Metric Tonnes			Imported as a % of Total
	Indigenous Production	Imported	Total	
2007-08	29.1	121.7	150.8	80.7
2008-09	27.9	132.8	160.7	82.6
2009-10	28.9	159.3	186.6	85.4
2010-11	33.3	163.2	196.5	83.1
2011-2012*	33.7	171.1	204.8	83.5

*Provisional Data

Source: Petroleum Planning and Analysis Cell (PPAC) Data quoted by Arvind Jayaram

Assessment: Indigenous production is stagnating, notwithstanding the recent finds in Cairn India's Rajasthan oil fields and Reliance KG D-6 oil fields.

As can be seen the import dependence is on the rise. However, while the consumption of oil has increased at the rate of 3.8 percent per annum, India's domestic production has remained relatively stagnant. (Planning Commission, n-1). Above findings have also been corroborated by the findings of the Energy Information Administration (EIA) of USA.

Figure-1.5

India oil production and consumption, 2001-2011
thousand barrels per day

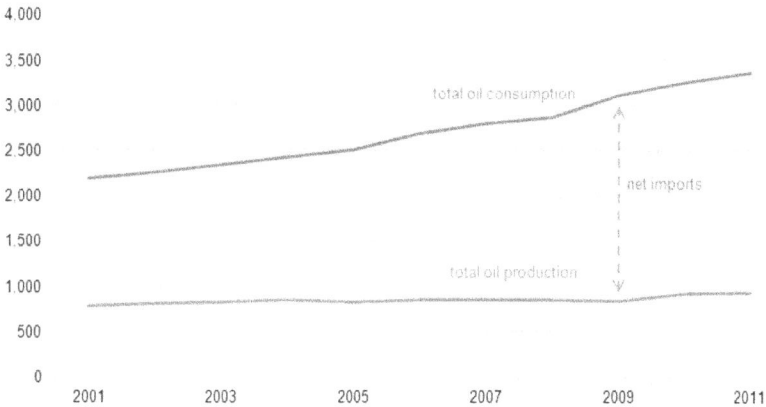

Source: U.S. Energy Information Administration, International Energy Statistics

The majority of India's oil goes to the transportation and industrial sectors, which consume 34 MTOE and 19.75 MTOE respectively. (Planning Commission, n-1). International Energy Outlook estimates that of the projected increase in oil demand during the next two decades, one half is expected to come in the transportation sector where there are not many competitive alternatives. There exists substantial concern that an oil-dependent India would not only drastically impact international supply but would further affect the oil prices in the world market.

Latest Indigenous Discoveries: Oil and Gas

Oil

- Cairn India discovered oil in the 26th oil Bearing structure in Rajastahan on 23 Mar 2013 and now the total capacity of the oil field increases from 300,000 barrels/day to 310,000 barrel/day. (Shine Jacob).

- ONGC discovered oil in D1 field of Mumbai High- 200 Kms West of Mumbai. It promises 60,000 barrels/ day. (Shuchi Srivastava).

Natural Gas-   RIL found oil in first well in five years in KG D-6 Basin. An additional column could be present in the MJ-1 exploration well in Dhirubhai-1 and 3 fields of KG-D6 block. (Shuchi Srivastava).

Natural Gas

"Natural gas has emerged as the most preferred fuel due to its inherent environmentally benign nature, greater efficiency and cost effectiveness. The demand of natural gas has sharply increased in the last two decades at the global level. In India too, the natural gas sector has gained importance, particularly over the last decade, and is being termed as the Fuel of the 21st Century."

- Ministry of Petroleum and Natural Gas, GOI.

Not only does the country have significant domestic reserves, but the cost of gas on the international market is significantly cheaper than that of oil. Moreover, gas is a multi-purpose fuel that can be used in power generation, but also for industry, fertilizer production, and domestic consumption. Part of the attraction of natural gas is the relative speed with which it can be exploited. Part of the attraction of natural gas is the relative speed with which it can be exploited. Whereas other sources of fuel take years to exploit, hydrocarbons can be sold in the market almost immediately. In this connection some of the useful stats is as follows:-

- Major hydro projects can take ten or fifteen years to build—and none of the pending projects are expected to go on-stream until 2015.

- Coal plants take four years to build. In addition the cost and time involved in developing an adequate integrated infrastructure also needs to be factored in. Because of the quality of Indian Coal (high ash content), there is a need to develop clean coal technology, which could take another decade before it is readily available in

India.

- Nuclear power is envisaged to play a large role in the long term, but it will take at least another thirty years before India reaches the level of the capability presently available in Europe or the US.

Thus, natural gas provides the perfect stop-gap solution which in view of the latest developments may finally become an important element of the India's energy security. Not only it is flexible in use (for industry, transportation and domestic use), it has relatively small smaller gestation period (12-18 months) for plants to come up. (Dr Sarbinder Singh).

Section-2: Policy Guidelines

Achieving an efficient configuration of the various forms of energy requires consistency in the policies governing each sector and consistency in the pricing of different types of energy. There is also a need for clarity in the direction in which we wish to move in aspects like energy security, research and development, addressing environmental concerns, energy conservation, etc. The energy policies that have been adopted since independence have encouraged and sustained much inefficiency in the use and production of energy. It needs to be appreciated that India pays one of the highest prices for energy in purchasing power parity terms. This has eroded the competitiveness of many sectors of the economy. The challenge is to ensure adequate supply of energy at the least possible cost. Another important challenge is to provide clean and convenient "lifeline" energy to every section of society, industry and security forces at a cost that is reasonable. Availability of energy affects the quality of life and as such the happiness index of the citizenry. Absence of this happiness quotient has an impact on the national strength and hence critical. Therein lies the importance of an effective and comprehensive Energy Policy. India faces formidable challenges in meeting its energy needs and in providing adequate energy of desired quality in various forms in a sustainable manner and at competitive prices. India needs to sustain an 8 percent to 10 percent economic growth rate, over the next 25 years, if it is to eradicate poverty and meet its human development goals. To deliver a sustained growth rate of 8 percent through 2031-32 and to meet the lifeline energy needs of all citizens, India needs, at the very least, to increase its primary energy supply by 3 to 4 times and, its electricity generation capacity/ supply by 5 to 6 times of their 2003-04 levels. With 2003-04 as the base, India's commercial energy supply would need to grow from 5.2 percent to 6.1 percent per annum while its total primary energy supply would need to grow at 4.3 percent to 5.1 percent annually. By 2031-32 power generation capacity must increase to nearly 8,00,000 MW from the current capacity of around 1,60,000 MW inclusive of all captive plants. Numerous policy reforms over the past 20 years have shifted India's energy sector from a predominantly government-owned system towards one based on market principles, offering a more level playing field for both public and private sectors. Political complexity and a tradition of socialist economic practices, however, hindered the complete liberalization of India's energy sector, leading to sub-optimal outcomes. In this sense, the huge blackouts that occurred in northern India in July 2012 could be seen as a consequence within the framework of incomplete market liberalization. (Sun-Joo Ahn and Dagmar Graczyk).

Increasing import dependency exposes India to greater geopolitical risks, fluctuating world Market prices and intensifying international competition. Indian energy policy cannot be set in isolation and needs to account for rising global interdependence, while simultaneously communicated appropriately to the public and reflected in policy debates.

India should overhaul its current patchwork of energy policies in favour of a comprehensive and clear-cut policy that encourages economic and social development through reliable energy supplies. There are a number of challenges that need to be addressed to create a well-functioning and financially-viable energy market in India. India should overhaul its current patchwork of energy policies in favour of a comprehensive and clear-cut policy that encourages economic and social development through reliable energy supplies.

Energy Policy Framework-   In India, the Energy Sector is essentially government controlled and most of the companies are in either in government sector or public sector. Therefore policy formulation & guidance and market regulation are controlled by the government. To grasp the intertwined dynamics in India's energy policy framework, comprehending not only the individual role of each ministry and government agency but also their interaction and coordination with other energy players is essential. Furthermore, some of the main ideas and themes that drive energy policy discourse in India should be taken into consideration. Presently this frame work to control energy resources from source to switch board is not well defined with lots of gaps. There Is a need to work out clear cut policy framework with institutional arrangements for coordination and key overarching policies for better management of the country's energy sector.

Policy objectives- There are three major policy objectives that India pursues: energy access, energy security and mitigation of climate change. All three objectives are closely related, but sometimes conflict with one another and are derived from the reality in India. Thus, it is challenging for India to maintain a balanced approach in pursuit of all three objectives.

Some of the important policies that guide the Indian energy scene are as elaborated in succeeding paragraphs.

Hydrocarbon Vision- 2025

India formulated a vision document namely; Hydrocarbon Vision 2025 towards the end of last Century with a perspective of period 2000-2025. The project was implemented with effect from the year 2000. It was set up to facilitate the future needs of India in the hydrocarbon sector. Hydrocarbon Vision 2025 would direct the policies related to hydrocarbon sector for next twenty five years. It would deal with energy security, use of alternative fuels, and inter-changeability of technology that would result in adequate quantities of economically priced clean and green fuels for Indian consumers. It, among other objectives, promises energy security by accomplishing self-reliance through indigenous production and investment in oil equity abroad. Hydrocarbon Vision 2025 aims at oil security; long-term sustainable supplies overseas; maintain self-sufficiency; sufficient storage of crude oil and petroleum product at different locations among others. Natural gas (NG) is emerging as the preferred fuel of the future in view of it being an environmental friendly economically attractive fuel and also a desirable feedstock. Increased focus needs to be given to this potential sector. The document has set following objectives for implementation:-

Objectives-

- To encourage use of natural gas. This may be noted that it is, relatively, a clean fuel.

- To ensure adequate availability by a mix of gas imports through pipelines and import of LNG.

- To tap unconventional sources of natural gas like Coal Bed Methane (CBM) natural gas hydrates, underground coal gasification (*Shale gas needs to be added to this list now; Author*) etc.

Strategy for Implementation-

- **Medium Term-**

  - Timely and continuous review of gas demand and supply options to facilitate policy interventions.

  - Pursuing diplomatic and political initiatives for import of gas from neighbouring and other countries with emphasis on transnational gas pipelines.

  - Expediting setting up of a regulatory framework.

  - Import LNG to supplement the domestic gas availability and encourage domestic companies to participate in the LNG chain.

  - Provide a level playing field for all the gas players and ensure reasonable transportation tariffs.

  - Rationalise customs duty on LNG and LNG projects.

  - Put in place an effective organisational structure, which would facilitate progress in the National Gas Hydrates Programme.

  - Opertionalise the Coal Bed Methane Policy with a time bound programme.

  - Formulate National Policy on Underground Coal Gasification in a time bound manner.

  - Increase R&D efforts on conversion of gas to liquids.

- **Long Term-**

  - Review of LNG option in the light of economic, political and energy security considerations.

  - Exploit the gas hydrates reserves.

  - Produce gas from CBM and through Underground Coal Gasification.

- Commercialize the production and use of alternate fuels like Di-Methyl Ether and use of Fuel Cells through increased R&P efforts. (*Acquisition of technology for exploitation of Shale Gas and also an assessment of its place in the Energy Security Matrix needs to be added to this list: Author*). (India Hydrocarbon Vision-2025 of the Government of India).

Integrated Energy Policy

A committee headed by Dr Kirit S Parikh, Member (Energy), Planning Commission of India has enunciated an integrated energy policy in 2005 which was adopted by the Government of India in 2008. This policy aims to bridge the prevailing gap in the demand and supply of energy in short, medium and long term perspective. Recognizing the role of both private and public sector participation in meeting the energy needs of the country, the policy strikes a right balance by stating that "wherever possible energy market should be competitive. The salient aspects of the policy, which are pertinent to the subject, are as follows:-

- Necessity of independent regulation across the entire energy spectrum.

- Pricing and resource allocation to be determined by market forces under an effective and credible regulatory oversight.

- Improved efficiencies across the energy chain.

- Policies that reflect externalities of energy consumption.

- Incentives / disincentives to regulate market and consumer behaviour.

- Management reforms to foster accountability and incentives for efficiency.

Vision of the Policy- The demand must be met through safe, clean and convenient forms of energy at the least-cost in a technically efficient, economically viable and environmentally sustainable manner to every section of the society. Considering the shocks and disruptions that can be reasonably expected, assured supply of such energy and technologies at all times is essential to provide energy security for all. Meeting this vision requires that India pursues all available fuel options and forms of energy, both conventional and non-conventional. Further, India must seek to expand its energy resource base and seek new and emerging forms of energy. Finally, and most importantly, India must pursue technologies that maximize energy efficiency, demand side management and conservation.

Some of the policy guidelines with respect to resources/ important forms of energy and other enabling provisions which need to be exploited to optimise the output energy sector as follows:-

- **Coal-** It is the view of the study that coal shall remain India's most important energy source till 2031-32 and possibly beyond. Thus, India must seek clean coal combustion technologies and, given the growing demand for coal, also pursue new coal extraction technologies such as in-situ gasification to tap its vast coal reserves that are difficult to extract economically using conventional technologies. Covering all coal bearing areas with comprehensive regional and detailed drilling could make a significant difference to the estimated life of India's coal reserves. India's extractable coal resources could be augmented through in-situ coal gasification which makes use of those coal deposits which are at greater depth and cannot be extracted economically by conventional methods. Extracting coal bed methane before and during mining could augment the country's energy resources. Policy stipulates that adequate Supply of Coal with Consistent Quality be ensured.

- **Ensuring Availability of Gas for Power Generation**: There is a total generation capacity of 12,604 MW based on gas and liquid fuels. Bulk of it is base loaded under combined cycle operation. However, gas supplies have been restricted and the overall utilization remains at only 54.5 percent. While requiring that no new gas capacity be built without firm and bankable gas supply agreements, effort should be made to allocate available domestic gas supplies to the fertilizer, petrochemicals, transport and power sectors at prices that are regulated to yield a fair return to domestic gas producers. Such a practice should be enforced till a better demand-supply balance emerges and domestic gas production achieves some of the potential that is often cited. A more competitive market can then function.

- **Power Sector Reforms:** These must focus on controlling the aggregate technical and commercial losses of the state transmission and distribution utilities. A robust and efficient inter-state and intra-state transmission system with adequate surplus capacity that is capable of transferring power from surplus regions to deficit regions is a must for ensuring optimal operation of the system.

- **Fuel Choices:** Integrated Energy Policy promotes efficient fuel choices and facilitates appropriate substitution.

- **Energy Efficiency and Demand Side Management**: Lowering the energy intensity of GDP growth through higher energy efficiency is important for meeting India's energy challenge and ensuring its energy security. The energy intensity of India's growth has been falling and is about half of what it used to be in the early seventies. Current figures and many sectoral studies confirm that there is room to improve and energy intensity can be brought down significantly in India with current commercially available technologies. Lowering energy intensity through higher efficiency is equivalent to creating a virtual source of untapped domestic energy and aggressive pursuit of energy efficiency and conservation, it is possible to reduce India's energy intensity by up to 25 percent from current levels. Efficiency can be increased in energy extraction, conversion, transportation, as well as in consumption.

Augmentation of Resources for Increased Energy Security:

India's energy resources can be augmented by exploration to find more coal, oil and gas, or by recovering a higher percentage of the in-place reserves. Developing the thorium cycle for nuclear power and exploiting non-conventional energy, especially solar power, offer possibilities for India's energy independence beyond 2050. Enhanced oil recovery and incremental oil recovery technologies could improve the proportion of in-place reserves that could be economically recovered from abandoned/

depleted fields. Isolated deposits of all hydro carbons including coal may be tapped economically through sub leases to the private sector.

Using Energy Abroad: In case India can access cheap natural gas overseas under long-term (25-30 years) arrangements, it should consider setting up captive fertiliser and/or gas liquefaction facilities in such countries. This would essentially augment energy availability for India.

Role of Nuclear and Hydro Power:

- Full realization of Hydro potential of the country by 2032. India has a potential of 1,50,000 MW capacity. The exploitation has been only to the extent of about 20 percent.

- Nuclear energy theoretically offers India the most potent means to long-term energy security. India has to succeed in realising the three-stage development process described in the main report and thereby tap its vast thorium resource to become truly energy independent beyond 2050. Continuing support to the three-stage development of India's nuclear potential is essential.

- Role of Renewable Energy: From a longer-term perspective and keeping in mind the need to maximally develop domestic supply options as well as the need to diversify energy sources, renewable energy continues to remain important to India's energy sector. It would not be out of place to mention that solar power could be an important player in India attaining energy independence in the long run. With a concerted push and a 40-fold increase in their contribution to primary energy, renewable may account for only 5 to 6 percent of India's energy mix by 2031-32. While this figure appears small, the distributed nature of renewable energy can provide many socio-economic benefits.

Ensuring Energy Security: India's energy security, at its broadest level, is primarily about ensuring the continuous availability of commercial energy at competitive prices to support its economic growth and meet the lifeline energy needs of its households with safe, clean and convenient forms of energy even if that entails directed subsidies. Reducing energy requirements and increasing efficiency are two very important measures to increase energy security. However, it is also necessary to recognise that

India's growing dependence on energy imports exposes its energy needs to external price shocks. Hence, domestic energy resources must be expanded. For India it is not a question of choosing among alternate domestic energy resources but exploiting all available domestic energy resources to the maximum as long as they are competitive. Ensuring energy security requires dealing with various risks. The threat to energy security arises not just from supply risks and the uncertainty of availability of imported energy, but also from possible disruptions or shortfalls in domestic production. Supply risks from domestic sources, such as from a strike in CIL or the Railways, also need to be addressed. Even if there is no disruption of supply, there can be the market risk of a sudden increase in energy price. Even when the country has adequate energy resources, technical failures may disrupt the supply of energy to some people. Generators could fail, transmission lines may trip or oil pipelines may spring a leak. One needs to provide security against such technical risks. Risks can be reduced by lowering the requirement of energy by increasing efficiency in production and use; by substituting imported fuels with domestic fuels; by diversifying fuel choices (gas, ethanol, orimulsion tar sands etc.) and supply sources; and by expanding the domestic energy resource base. Risks can also be dealt with by increasing the ability to withstand supply shocks through creation of strategic reserves, the ability to import energy and face market risk by building hard currency reserves and by providing redundancy to address technical risks. Following has been recommended: Maintain a reserve, equivalent to 90 days of oil imports for strategic-cum-buffer stock purposes and/or buy options for emergency supplies from neighbouring large storages such as those available in Singapore. Since 80 percent of global hydrocarbon reserves are controlled by national oil companies controlled by respective governments, oil diplomacy establishing bilateral economic, social and cultural ties can reduce supply risk.

Boosting Energy Related R&D: Demonstrations of new technologies, their economic assessment and further R&D to make the new technology acceptable and attractive to customers could follow, before finally leading to commercialisation and diffusion. Some key policy initiatives relevant to energy related R&D are detailed below:-

- A National Energy Fund (NEF) should be set-up to finance energy R&D.

- A number of technology missions should be mounted for developing near-commercial technologies and rolling out new technologies in a time bound manner. These include coal technologies (where India should focus) for efficiency improvement; in-situ gasification; IGCC and carbon sequestration; solar technologies covering solar- thermal and photovoltaics; bio-fuels such as bio-diesel and ethanol; bio-mass plantation and wood gasification, and community based bio-gas plants.

- **Provision of Cooking Energy**: We may set a goal to provide clean cooking energy such as LPG, NG, biogas or kerosene to all within 10 years. The total amount of LPG required to provide cooking energy to 1.5 billion persons is around 55 Mtoe.

- Per capita availability of electricity to be increased to over 1000 units by 2012.

12th Plan Strategy With Respect to Petroleum Products

Demand of petroleum products is projected to increase at an annual rate of 4.7 percent during the Twelfth Five Year Plan. This will increase consumption of POL products from 147.98 MMT in 2011–12 to 186.21 MMT by 2016–17. (Sec 14.167 of the 12th Plan Document.). Oil production during Twelfth Plan is likely to increase marginally and then decline by 3.26 percent by the end of the Plan resulting into higher import dependence (Sec 14.168 of 12th Plan Document.) This aspect has already been analysed in an earlier section. The demand of natural gas during the Twelfth Plan is likely to grow by about 19.2 percent to meet the incremental requirement of power, fertiliser and other industries. The CNG and city gas sector will also see a quantum growth in natural gas use. It is expected that by the end of the Twelfth Plan, about 300 cities are likely to be covered under city gas distribution. (Sec 14.169 of 12th Plan Document).

Domestic production of natural gas during the Twelfth Plan will depend upon the output from gas fields discovered under New Exploration licensing Policy (NELP) by various operators. As majority of new gas prospects are in deep water, the investments, technology and pricing of gas for developing these fields would be important. (Sec 14.170, 12th Plan Document). However the domestic production will need to augment by import/ acquisition of gas equity abroad or through Trans-national pipe lines to meet the domestic demands. The immediate need for import is as tabulated below:-

Table-2.1

Quantity of Natural Gas to Be Imported

	Production	Consumption	Import	Proved Reserve
Natural Gas	46.1 BCM (2011 estimate)	61.1 BCM (2011 estimate)	12.15 BCM (2011 estimate)	1.154 TCM

Source: CIA's Country Fact Book updated up to 08 April 2013 and uploaded on http://www.cia.gov/library/publications/the-world-factbook/geos/in.html

Section-3: Structure of the Brief

Terms of Reference

Having accepted the centrality of the Natural Gas in the energy basket for India in short to medium time span an attempt needs to be made to examine its viability for its indigenous sourcing and measures to augment its quantum to meet the future needs.

Presently the import of the natural gas is from Middle East, North Africa, Europe and some of the Caribbean countries. However close to India some of the countries/ regions; abundantly rich in natural gas exist. These are; Central Asian republics, Caspian Rim countries and Iran. Issues entailed in getting gas from these countries need examination. However the transportation of resources from these countries is through some of the most volatile geographies and also certain geo-political issues have a direct bearing on the passage of gas, which need examination.

Finally certain new technological breakthroughs have emerged as the game changers in the world energy management. It needs to be examined whether India can benefit from them and if so how?

Aim

To examine the role of Pakistan in India's Energy security Matrix and alternative options which can be gone in to enhance the state of India's Energy Security.

Scope

Based on the background already deliberated earlier in the paper following issues are being examined:-

- Growth of India's natural gas sector.

- Status of transnational gas pipelines; Turkmenistan-Afghanistan-Pakistan-India (TAPI) and Iran-Pakistan-India (IPI)

- Impact of breakthrough in shale gas technology in USA on international energy market.

- An assessment of Indian preparedness/ planning to exploit the emerging scenario.

- Other options for India to enhance the energy supply.

Section-4: Growth of Natural Gas Sector In India

According to the *Oil & Gas Journal*, India had 43.8 Trillion Cubic Feet (TCF) of proved natural gas reserves at the end of 2012. About 30 percent of these are onshore reserves, while 70 percent are offshore reserves. In 2002, energy companies made a number of large gas discoveries in the Krishna-Godavari (KG) basin off India's Eastern coast, pushing up both the reserve base and production.es. The indigenous production is steadily rising. From **88.8 Million Metric Standard Cubic Meters per Day** (MMSCMD) at the beginning 11th Plan (2007-08), it has gone up to 130 MMSCMD in 2011-12 with a spike of 143.1 MMSCMD in 2010-11. It was due to sudden drop in the production from KG D-6 of Reliance (Out of 22 wells nine have gone dry). (Discussion at the Ministry of Petroleum and Natural Gas (MoP&NG) on 09 Apr 2013) and though the domestic production is rising but so is the **demand at the rate of 10 percent since 2001.** The power sector and fertilizer sector make up the majority of natural gas demand in 2010 at 45 percent and 28 percent, respectively. The government labeled these as priority sectors, which ensures that they receive larger shares of any new gas supply before other consumers. (EIA)

India has become importer of Gas since 2004. In 2011, India consumed 2.3 TCF. The MoP&NG projects, that if this trend continues, India's gas demand is likely to become more than double in next five years. Such a rise in demand is likely to increase the import dependence (EIA).

Figure-4.1

India natural gas production and consumption, 2001-2011
billion cubic feet

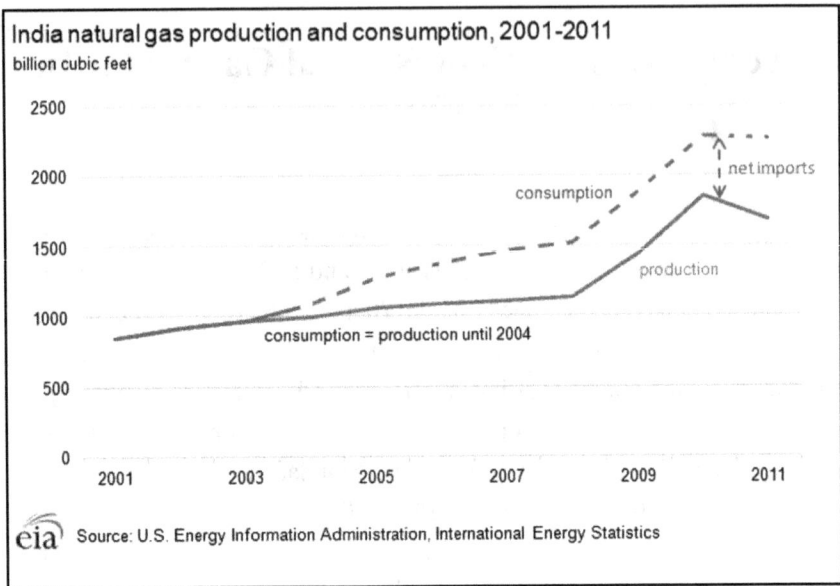

Source: U.S. Energy Information Administration, International Energy Statistics

The gap between demand and supply is likely to become even more in coming years which will further increase the need for import:-

Table-4.1

Rising Import Dependency (In MMSCMD)

Year	2012-13	2013-14	2014-15	2015-16	2016-17
Total availability from domestic sources	117	120	129	139.2	175.08
Projected demand	293	371	405	446	473
Dependence on R-LNG Assuming entire demand to be met	176	251	276	306	297
Import dependency%	60.06	67.65	68.14	68.6	62.79

Note:

- The dip in quantity is due to drop in production in KG-D-6 basin of Reliance Gas Field and Syria and Sudan gas fields of OVL not producing their optimum due to internal situation there and rise in 2016-17 is based on the assumption that the new gas fields acquired by OVL including Kazakhstan and Mozambique (BS Reporters). Even KG D-6 is expected to produce more.

- Source of supply are Trinidad & Tobago, Equatorial Guinea, Russia, Qatar, Abu Dhabi, Norway, Oman, Egypt, Nigeria, Algeria, Yemen, Spain etc.

- To ensure security of supply, sources of supply, as can be seen are quite diversified (Indian Oil companies are present in 22 countries) (Sec 2.3.4 of Energy security Hand Book) and in addition a number of other business models are being pursued.

Source: Discussion at Ministry of Petroleum and Natural gas Government of India, MEA and OVL.

Pipeline Network- Although a reasonably large pipeline network Within India is being operated by Gas Authority of India Limited (GAIL), Reliance Gas Transportation Infrastructure (RGTIL), Petronet and Assam Gas Company but an insufficient pipeline infrastructure constrains natural gas demand in India. In recent times an effort is on to establish new pipelines to connect gas fields to industrial centres (EIA).

Figure-4.2

Gas Pipeline Network within India

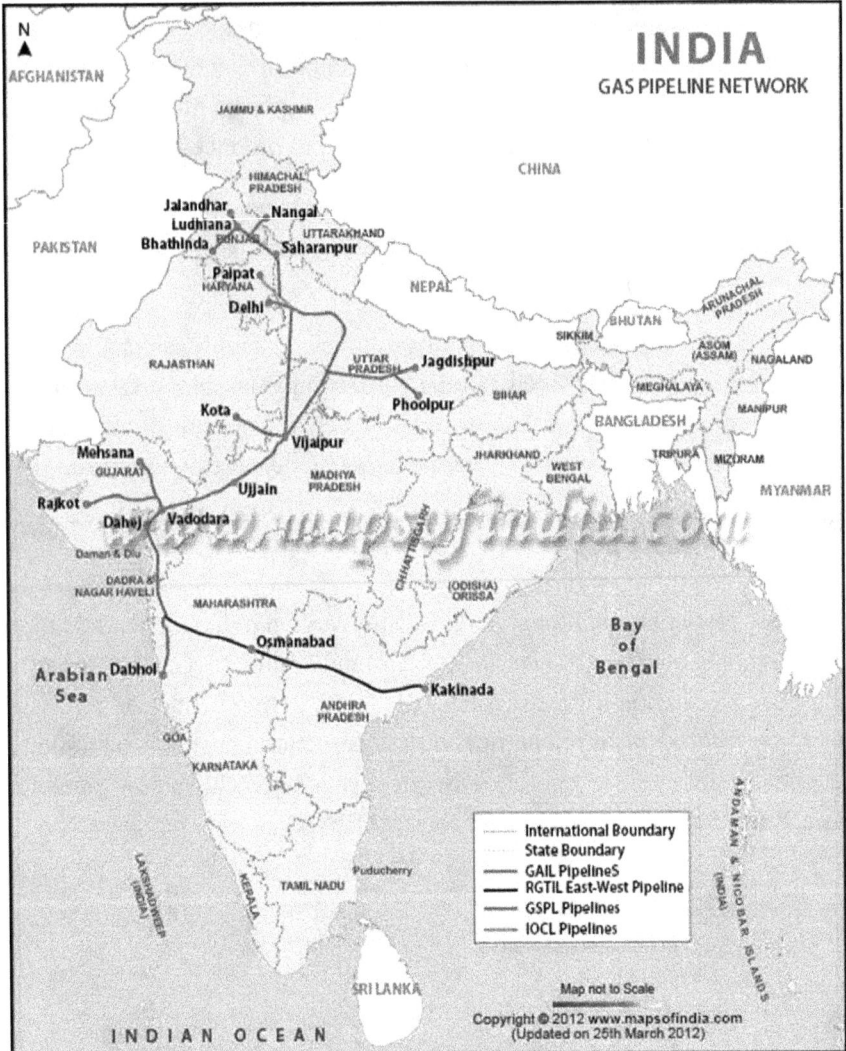

Natural Gas Imports- India's natural gas import demand is expected to increase in the coming years. To help meet this growing demand, a number of import schemes including both LNG and pipeline projects have either been implemented or considered.

Section-5: Sources of Natural Gas for India from West

There are a large number of countries are producing natural gas as is evident from following bar chart. However for our discussion of the subject only those countries in this section will be considered which are located towards the west of India.

Figure-5.1

Top Global Natural Gas Reserves by Country. January 1, 2012

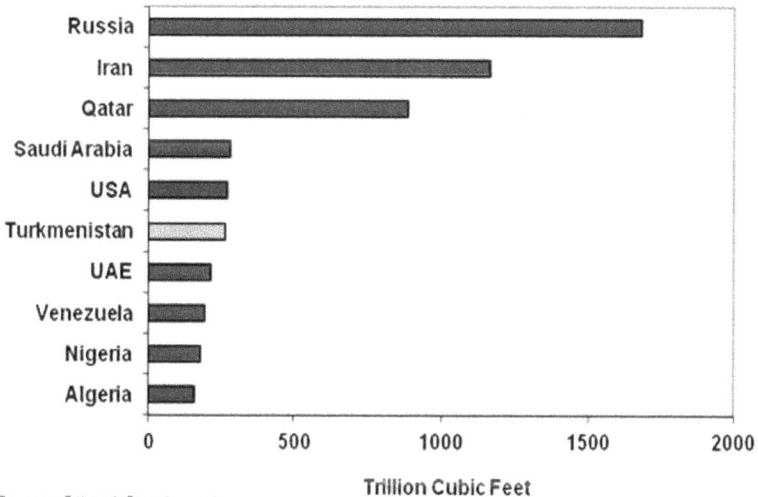

Caspian Sea Rim Nations- According to the BP Statistical Review of World Energy (2004), proven oil reserves of the five Caspian littoral states total 216.4 billion barrels, while total gas reserves are estimated at 2819.2 TCF. In terms of percentages, the five Caspian littoral states have about 18.8 percent of the world's total proven oil reserves and 45 percent of the world's total proven gas reserves (Mehdi Parvizi Amineh and Henk Houweling). Officials and analysts from the U.S. Energy Information Agency stated in 2004 that the world's unproven oil reserves are expected to double in the next two decades. States located in the former Soviet Union are likely to account for a projected fourfold increase (Guy F Caruso and Linda E. Doman). As such, there should be no doubt that total Caspian oil and gas reserves are set to be adjusted upwards in the coming years, where the major share of this increase will flow from Kazakhstan, Turkmenistan and Azerbaijan. Meanwhile, the proportion of the Caspian region's energy exports as a share of total world energy supply has increased. In 2001, the five Caspian littoral states exported a total of about 9.2 trillion barrels of oil and 12.05 TCF of natural gas to the international market, but exports are estimated to increase to 31.5 trillion barrels of oil and 41.5 TCF of natural gas by 2010 (Mehdi Parvizi Amineh and Henk Houweling, PP: 87-88). The importance of Central Asian region has been well articulated by Svante E. Cornell:

> *"With strategic access crucial to the prosecution of the war [on terror], the republics of Central Asia took centre stage in the most important conflict to confront the United States in decades. Although less prominently covered in the media, the states of the South Caucasus were equally vital; situated between Iran and Russia, they were the only practical corridor connecting NATO territory with Central Asia and Afghanistan."*

Turkmenistan- Currently ranks in the top six countries for natural gas reserves and the top 20 in terms of gas production. According to Oil & Gas Journal (*OGJ*), Turkmenistan has proven natural gas reserves of approximately 265 TCF in 2012, a significant increase from 94 TCF estimated in 2009. Turkmenistan has several of the world's largest gas fields, including 10 with over 3.5 TCF of reserves located primarily in the Amu Darya basin in the South East, the Murgab Basin, and the South Caspian basin in the west. Recent major discoveries at South Yolotan in the prolific eastern part of the country are expected to offset most declines in other large, mature gas fields and will likely add to the current proven reserve amounts. Despite vast gas reserves, limited export and investment options pose challenges to monetizing and producing gas resources. A majority of Turkmen gas travels to Russia where it is consumed or transits through Russia to end markets in Europe. Since 1992, Russia, the key export market for Turkmenistan, has exerted significant influence over export prices of gas resources charged by the Central Asian state. As a result of a pipeline explosion on the Central Asian Center export pipeline to Russia in April 2009, Turkmen gas production was shut in and suffered serious declines. Gas production fell almost 50 percent from a high of 2.5 TCF per annum in 2008 to 1.3 TCF per annum in 2009. Following the pipeline repair and a new pricing agreement signed with Russia in January 2010, Turkmenistan raised production to 1.6 TCF per annum in 2010. However, Russia agreed to accept about 400 BCF per annum or only one-third of the volumes it imported prior to the explosion and at a lower import price, resulting from its declining exports to Europe.

Figure-5.2

Turkmenistan's Potential for export

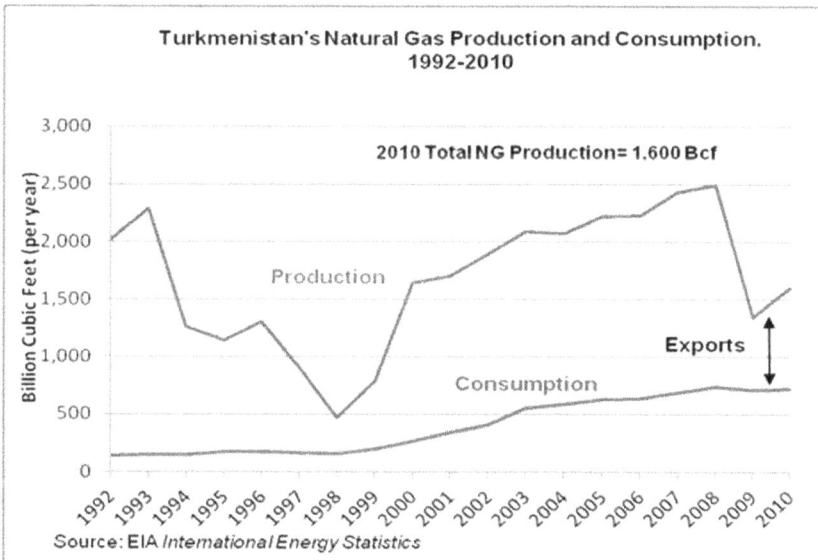

Turkmenistan is seeking ways to boost gas production as well as release the current shut-in gas volume by diversifying its portfolio of export markets. Turkmenistan plans to increase production as exports are likely to materialize via new pipelines being planned to China and Iran. Also another pipeline is being planned to connect the gas fields of Turkmenistan to India via Afghanistan and Pakistan. One fact which needs to be taken into account is that Turkmenistan though has large amount of natural gas reserves but is constrained by the lack of gas transportation infrastructure.

Figure-5.3

Gas Pipeline Network in Central Asian Region, Iran and Middle East

The Dauletabad field, located in the Amu Darya basin in the southeast, is one of Turkmenistan's largest and oldest gas-producing fields with estimated reserves of 60 TCF. The field produced approximately 1.2 TCF per annum in 2010 or most of Turkmenistan's gas supply, however, production is declining. CNPC is the only foreign company with direct access to an onshore development, the Bagtyiarlyk project near the Amu Darya River, through a 35-year production sharing agreement. The project came online at the end of 2009 with a capacity of 182 Billion cubic feet (BCF) per year and began feeding gas to the Central Asia China pipeline.

By 2012, the field is expected to ramp up production capacity to 460 BCF per year to supply gas to China. In 2006, Turkmenistan announced the discovery of the South Yolotan deposit, located in the South Eastern Murgab Basin north of the Dauletabad field. An independent audit estimated in October 2011 that the field's potential reserves are at least 460 TCF and possibly as high as 740 TCF, which would make South Yolotan the second largest field in the world. In order to aid in financing the field development, the China Development Bank provided a $4 billion loan in 2009 for the project's first phase of development, and, in 2011, pledged another $4.1 billion for the second phase. Industry analysts expect the field to be online by 2013 and to export gas via the Central Asia-China Pipeline. The Turkmen government is open to foreign investment and ownership in oil and gas fields in the country's offshore section of the Caspian Sea. Most gas from the Caspian Sea is associated with oil production and is currently flared until companies can monetize the supply. Petronas and Dragon Oil produce gas through their respective PSAs in the Diyarbekir (Block 1) and Cheleken fields. Petronas currently flares gas from Block 1 while the company seeks ways to commercialize production. Turkmengaz signed a gas purchase agreement in July 2011 with Petronas, and Malaysia and Turkmenistan signed a cooperation agreement enabling Petronas to build a 360 Bcf/y-capacity gas processing plant on the Caspian coast to receive the gas from Block 1. (Country Analysis Brief: Turkmenistan by Energy Information Administration of USA)

Iran-   Iran is one of the richest regions in the world in terms of hydrocarbon resources. Iran has a well developed exploration and production programme which has a long history of over a century. Iran's gas reserves represent the equivalent of about 216 billion barrels (3.43×1010 CUM) of oil Equivalent. Iran still has huge potential for new significant gas discoveries: areas like Caspian Sea, North East, Central Kavir and especially areas starting from Aghar and Dalan gas fields in Fars province up to the Strait of Hormuz] and Central Persian Gulf have considerable amount of undiscovered gas resources (Undiscovered Oil and Gas Resources of Lower Silurian Qusaiba-Paleozoic Total Petroleum Systems). USGS estimates that Iran's undiscovered gas resources could be 200–800 trillion cubic feet (5.7×1012–23×1012 CUM) (USGS, World Conventional Gas Resources, by Basin). The Permo-Triassic successions (the Dehram group in Iran and its lateral equivalent, the Khuff formation), are major gas-producing intervals in these basins.

Figure-5.4

Natural Gas Assets of Iran

The supergiant North Dome/South Pars field alone is estimated to hold about 19 percent of the world's total gas reserves, producing gas and condensate from these intervals (Behrooz Esrafili-Dizaji and Hossain Rahimpur-Bonab). There are 43 Gas Fields and there are 92 natural gas reservoirs. According to Iran Energy Balance Sheet (2009, in Persian), 78 of these fields are currently active, with 62 onshore and 16 offshore, leaving 67 fields inactive at present. Some 23 hydrocarbon fields lie in border areas and are shared between Iran and adjacent countries, including Kuwait, Iraq, Qatar, Bahrain, UAE, Saudi Arabia and Turkmenistan . (Behrooz Esrafili-Dizaji, Farkhondeh Kiani Harchegani).

Figure-5.5

Iran: Production pattern: Oil and Natural Gas

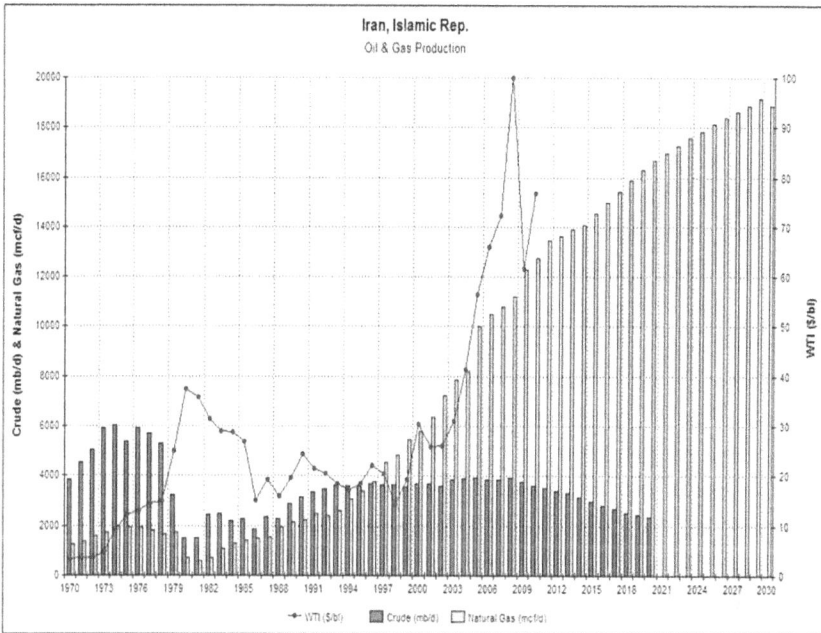

Iran also has substantial amount of Natural gas reserve to spare for export. In recent years the natural gas production is showing a steady rise (refer Figure-11). *Therefore it becomes amply clear that for India's energy security energy bearing resources available in Central Asian region and Iran are of vital importance due to their proximity, spare capacity of the host countries to spare the gas for export and a good potential for developing interdependence between the host countries (Iran and CARs) and the country needing energy (India).*

Section-6: Centrality of Pakistan in India's Energy Matrix

The geographical location of Pakistan makes it extremely important in any plan wherein a land based engagement for transportation of energy is considered either with Central Asia or with Iran. Therefore it would be of relevance if the state economy of Pakistan is analysed to appreciate her capacity to support her efforts to create infrastructure for energy import and also her state of domestic production of energy is analysed to appreciate the need for energy import.

State of Economy- Decades of internal political disputes and low levels of foreign investment have led to slow growth and underdevelopment in Pakistan. Agriculture accounts for more than one-fifth of output and two-fifths of employment. Textiles account for most of Pakistan's export earnings, and Pakistan's failure to expand a viable export base for other forms of manufacturing has left the country vulnerable to shifts in world demand. Official unemployment is under 6 percent, but this fails to capture the true picture, because much of the economy is informal and underemployment remains high. Over the past few years, low growth and high inflation, led by a spurt in food prices, have increased the amount of poverty - the UN Human Development Report estimated poverty in 2011 at almost 50 percent of the population. Inflation has worsened the situation, climbing from 7.7 percent in 2007 to almost 12 percent for 2011, before declining to 10 percent in 2012. As a result of political and economic instability, the Pakistani rupee has depreciated more than 40 percent since 2007. The government agreed to an International Monetary Fund Standby Arrangement in November 2008 in response to a balance of payments crisis. Although the economy has stabilized since the crisis, it has failed to recover. Foreign investment has not returned, due to investor concerns related to governance, energy, security, and a slow-down in the global economy. Remittances from overseas workers, averaging about $1 billion a month since March 2011, remain a bright spot for Pakistan.

However, after a small current account surplus in fiscal year 2011 (July 2010/June 2011), Pakistan's current account turned to deficit in fiscal year 2012, spurred by higher prices for imported oil and lower prices for exported cotton. Pakistan remains stuck in a low-income, low-growth trap, with growth averaging about 3% per year from 2008 to 2012. It emerges that Pakistan needs to address long standing issues related to government revenues and energy production in order to spur the amount of economic growth that will be necessary to employ its growing population. Other long term challenges include expanding investment in education and healthcare, and reducing dependence on foreign donors. (Index Mundi Feb 2013)

Table-6.1

Pakistan: State Of Economy

GDP at Purchasing Power parity (2012 Estimate)	$ 514.6 billion	Year on year growth- 1.03%
GDP at official exchange rate	$ 230.5 billion	Real Growth Rate- 3.7% (2011 estimate)
Budget Revenues: Expenditures:	$29.51 billion $44.19 billion (2012 est.)	
Inflation rate 2011 estimates: 2012 estimates:	11.3% 11.9%	Based on consumer prices
Current Account Balance 2011 estimates: 2012estimates:	$268 million -$4.632 billion	
Exports 2011 estimates: 2012 estimates:	$26.3 billion $24.66 billion	

| Imports 2011 estimates: 2012 estimates: | $38.93 billion $40.82 billion | |
| Reserves of foreign exchange and gold 2011 estimates: 2012 estimates: | $18.09 billion $13.5 billion | As on 31 Dec 2011 As on 30 Nov 2012 |

Note: As can be seen almost all parameters are falling and the economy has hardly any intrinsic strength to support any major infrastructure project on its own without getting external support. Such a state makes the Country quite vulnerable to international pressures while taking decision with respect to projects on Energy.

Source: Index Mundi with inputs from CIA World Fact Book updated up to Feb 2013.

Table-6.2

Pakistan: State of Energy Assets
(Only Petroleum Based Assets)

Asset	Production	Consumption	Proven Reserve
Crude Oil	63.08 bbl/day (2011 estimate)	246.08 bbl/day (2009 estimate	480.9 million bbl (Jan 2013 estimate)
Natural Gas	42.9 BCM (2011 estimate)	42.9 BCM (2011 estimate)	753 8 BCM (Jan 2012 estimate)

Source: The CIA World Fact Book uploaded on https://www.cia.gov/library/publications/the-world-factbook/

Assessment:

- The economy does not have enough intrinsic strength to support a trans-national pipeline without an external support, in case that terminates at Pakistan.

- Pakistan is terribly short of energy and does need massive infusion of capital investment to upgrade energy infrastructure.

Energy Outlook of Pakistan (2010/11 to 2025/26)

Background-   Natural gas production in Pakistan is at a relatively high level presently and remaining reserves are estimated to be about 885.3 BCM (1 January 2009 estimates). Pakistan's gas fields are only expected to last for about another 20 years at the most due to heavy industrial usage (Trading Chart.com and Pakistan petroleum Website). The Sui gas field is the biggest natural gas field in Pakistan. It is located near Sui in Balochistan. The gas field was discovered in the late 1952 and the commercial exploitation of the field began in 1955. Sui gas field accounts for 26 percent of Pakistan's gas production (Anthea Pitt).   Remaining reserves are estimated to be at about 800 BCF and the daily production is around 660 million cubic feet (MCF) of natural gas. The operator of the field is Pakistan Petroleum Limited.   Pipeline net work in Balochistan has been quite vulnerable to sabotage by secessionist groups like the Balochistan Liberation Front and/ or Balochistan Liberation Army since the year 2000.   In recent times it has been assessed by a number of agencies that the Federally Administered Tribal Areas of Pakistan (FATA) and Frontier Regions (FR) are believed to be having massive reserves of oil and natural gas—which Pakistani officials have suddenly become very keen to explore. (Farooq Tirmizi) But this is a highly restive, war-torn area where one right move could make all the difference, and one wrong move could ignite a conflict with irreversible consequences. For now, the area remains unexplored and it was only in 2008 when Pakistani geologists began to study the area in earnest, with the support of the local authorities in FATA and the FR. The results of this research were collected, processed and digitized in June 2012. The geologists discovered seven new oil and gas seepages during the mapping. The geologists also claim that 11 oil and gas exploration companies have already reserved 16 blocks in FATA (*Upstream Online*)

Figure-6.1

Pakistan: Excessive Dependence on Declining Natural Gas for Energy Security

PAKISTAN ENERGY CONSUMPTION   FIG. 2

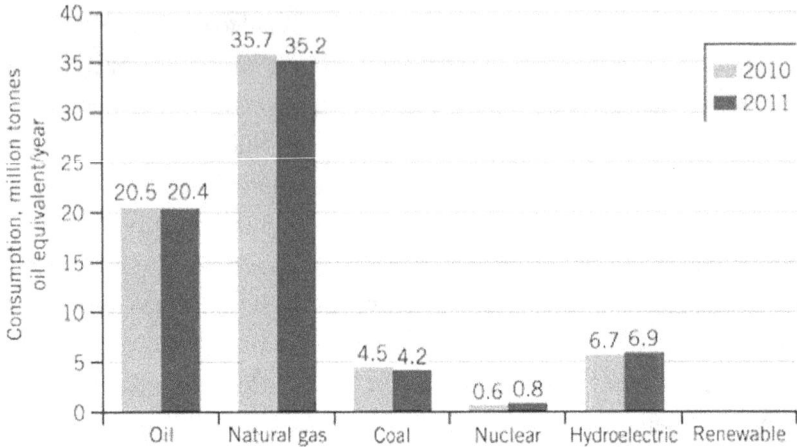

Source: BP Statistical Review of World Energy 2012

Pakistan's energy sector is in a state of crisis and over the past few years has negatively impacted the social and economic development of the country. Primary energy consumption in Pakistan has grown by almost 80 percent over the past 15 years, from 34 MTOE in 1994/95 to 61 MTOE in 2009/10 and has supported an average GDP growth rate in the country of about 4.5 percent per annum. However since 2006-07 energy supply has been unable to meet the country's demand leading to shortages. Meanwhile per capita energy consumption in Pakistan at under 0.5 TOE/ capita remains only one-third of world average. Pakistan's domestic gas production is expected to fall from the current 4 BCFPD to 2 BCFPD by 2020. Demand, on the other hand, is expected to soar to 8 BCFPD by that time, creating a shortfall of 6BCFPD (A 'The Express Tribune' Report dated 14 Mar 2011). If every project that Pakistan is currently planning – including a pipeline from Iran, large offshore gas import terminals, and even the politically dicey pipeline from Turkmenistan that passes through Afghanistan – were to be completed on time and deliver exactly as much gas as expected, the country will still be short of 2 BCFPD in 2020 (IBID).

An Analysis of Demand Side Management of the Gas- Demand growth is expected to outpace increase in supply, and gas shortages may intensify in the near future. Based on supply projections, domestic production of gas is likely to peak by FY14 at 3,860 MMCFPD and is set to decline thereafter. Natural depletion in gas fields will ensure that committed supplies fall considerably short of demand, which is projected to reach 5,970 MMCFPD by FY16. Production from fields presently identified for development will therefore become critical in managing the demand-supply gap. Key projects scheduled to come online by FY14 will contribute 460 MMCFPD to gas supplies. Furthermore, since domestic production of gas will no longer be sufficient to meet consumption requirements, reliance on imports will increase. Between FY12 and FY16, the domestic gas shortfall is projected to increase from 2,458 MMCFPD to 3,021 MMCFPD, which may be reduced by 40 percent via imports. Pakistan is left with only 50 percent natural gas reserves as high consumption in different sectors has exhausted 50 percent of the overall reserves of 54 TCF by financial year of 2011-12, (Annual report of State Bank of Pakistan: 2011-12).The country now has barely enough resources to last for just over 20 years, under the increasingly unlikely scenario that current production rates are maintained throughout. The country experienced some of the worst gas shortages in its history in 2011 as supply to the industrial, compressed natural gas (CNG) and power sectors was significantly curtailed, resulting in closure of hundreds of units and losses to business and productions (A 'Daily Times' report dated 28 Dec 2011).

An appraisal of Indigenous Sources of Pakistan- Indigenous natural gas has been the largest source of energy supply in Pakistan contributing 27.7 MTOE (45.4 percent) in 2009/10, followed by oil products, mainly imports, at 21.3 MTOE (34.9 percent), hydro power at 7.5 MTOE (12.3 percent), coal, mainly imports, at 3.7 MTOE (6.1 percent) and nuclear power at 0.8 MTOE (1.3 percent). Consumption of indigenous natural gas has grown rapidly in all sectors of the economy (residential, commercial, industrial, transport and power) over the past 15 years, driven by growing availability of gas and a low, government-controlled gas price as compared with alternate fuel prices. As a result, Pakistan has developed a vast natural gas transmission and distribution infrastructure across the country. However Pakistan's indigenous natural gas reserves are declining rapidly. If current gas policies persist, Pakistan's natural gas supply is expected to decline from 4 BCF per day (BCFD) in 2010/11 to less than 1 BCFD by 2025/26. This will lead to a growing gas/energy shortfall reaching 8 BCFD (over 50 MTOE) by 2025/26 and will depress Pakistan's average GDP growth rate over the next 15 years. Thus there is a need for increased emphasis on domestic exploration, or large scale import; either through liquefied natural gas (LNG) route or through regional gas pipelines. It is also unlikely that Pakistan will be able to substantially develop its other indigenous energy sources consisting of hydro power due to acute shortage of water availability within the country and thermal power due to current policies by 2025/26. Therefore a very serious energy scenario of import dependency rising from present 30 percent to 75 percent costing over $ 50 billion per annum in foreign exchange by 2025-26 stares in its face. (Asma Shakir Khwaja). In the absence of even a single LNG terminal, a highly expensive proposition, Pakistan does not have a choice but to go for augmenting the natural gas supply through regional pipelines. However on its own Pakistan would find it difficult to get these gas pipelines constructed and there after manage them due to high cost involved. Therefore it would be in Pakistan's interest if she manages to get India involved in these international pipelines as equal parents because such an approach will not only will reduce the cost of infrastructure build up but will also help Pakistan to earn some much needed dollars as transit tariff. It will be a win-win situation for both India and Pakistan and will result into an interdependence which will ensure safety and security of the pipeline.

Figure-6.2

Two Proposed Pipelines in South Asia

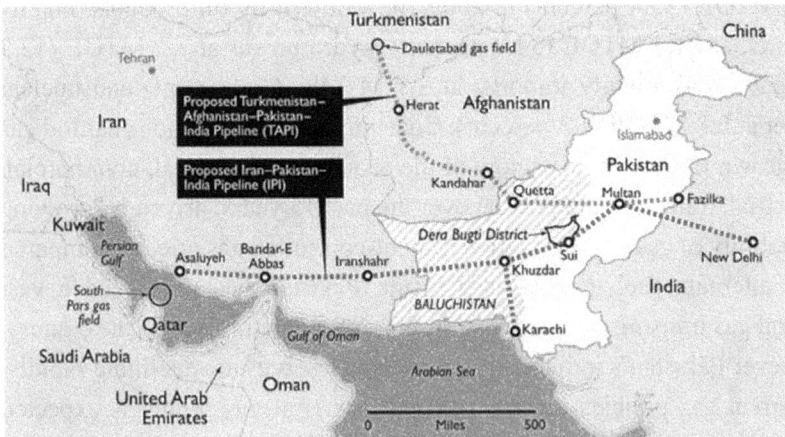

Map 1 · B 2139 ⚡ heritage.org

Safety and Security of the Assets- However, safety and security of these pipelines which will be transiting through some of the most volatile areas in the region will be an issue which will have to be addressed by the respective holders with respect to their respective areas. Alternatively an institutionalized international protection force will have to be planned under the aegis of the agency which will be entrusted to run these pipelines. In such a situation the cost of safety and security of the assets will have to be factored in.

Geopolitical Interests having Bearing on these Projects-

- In this connection an important issue is the US interest. If these pipelines come up based on commercial interests and through regional cooperation, which probably would be in the best interests of the stake holders but due a very a capital investment needed, involvement of the world financial institutions may become imperative. It is a well known secret such a trajectory will need the support of USA, the lone Super power of the world. It is appreciated that a heightened regional cooperation may not be in the interest of the USA as in such a situation their leverage would be quite limited. It goes without saying that it is possible that US may try to control these assets as a part of its strategy of 'War on Terror' as a hidden agenda of securing the control over oil and gas reserves of the region. In such a situation, the Iran-Pakistan Gas Pipeline project is likely to become the first casualty because US is conscious of the fact that they will not have adequate leverage on Iran and therefore all their effort will be to ensure that this project does not see the light of the day. However, pipeline from Turkmenistan is relatively has better chance of success. In this connection a statement by US Ambassador to Pakistan at the Lahore University of Management Sciences (LUMS) on November 25, 2011 is quite significant, wherein he said that "*Pak-Iran gas pipeline is not a good idea....however, the plan to get gas from Turkmenistan is a better idea,*". (Huzaima Bukhari and Dr Ikramul Haq). In a way it was a mere reiteration of the economic interests of the United States and its allies. The statement, in effect, has serious political connotations that relate to an area that has always been the battlefield of the Great Game. The Pakistan government reacted strongly against Cameron Munter's statement, saying, *"Islamabad will not accept any dictation regarding its internal affairs from any foreign country. Gas from Iran is in the country's best interest."* (Huzaima Bukhari and Dr Ikramul Haq).

- After India's pullout from the Iran-Pakistan gas pipeline project (IP), following its civil nuclear deal with the US, both China and Russia have shown interest in the project. The Russian gas-export monopoly, Gazprom and CNPC have promised to help build the 780-kilometer pipeline. It is worrisome for the US and its allies that China and US is of the view that the cooperation by Russia and China to IP pipeline project will harm her vital geopolitical interests. Main interests of China and Russia are that they see an opportunity to break the monopoly on financial issues of the giant Western Oil and Natural gas companies.

- As far as US-Iran relations are concerned US has still not been able to come out of her traditional mistrust of Iran, post Islamic Revolution of 1979, which has further been hardened due to Iranian efforts to acquire nuclear status which US perceives as nuclear weponization effort of Iran and as such her Endeavour is to strangulate Iran through economic sanctions, drying up of funding of developmental projects in Iran through world financial institutions like IMF and World Bank which US and her Western allies control.

Pak Interests in IP and TAPI- Pakistan's Pakistan Federal Minister for Petroleum and Natural Resources, Dr. Asim Hussain, in a TV interview in October 2011, said: "Our dependence on Pak-Iran pipeline is very high and there is no other substitute at present to meet the growing demand of energy." (IBID) This statement irritated the Unites States, which has been pleading the case for the Turkmenistan Gas project (TAPI) since the 1990s. TAPI was initially designed to provide Turkmen gas to Pakistan through Afghanistan. In April 2008, India was also invited to join. Pakistan's cabinet gave approval to the Gas Pipeline Framework Agreement (GPFA) for TAPI in its meeting on October 27, 2010. On November 13, 2011, Pakistan and Turkmenistan initiated the Gas Sales and Purchase Agreement

(GSPA), which is likely to bring the multi-nation project into operation by 2016.

Iran's Interest- Iran wants to diversify gas sales to Asian markets and Asian countries basically to earn revenue for the resources that she has surplus to her requirement and also to break the pariah status being forced on her by the USA. Tehran's projection of IP as a peace pipeline has the support of Russia and China. While regional powers desire to find a stable, reliable source of gas supplies, America and its allies want to destabilize the entire region using militancy as a tool of foreign policy. The tussle over IP and TAPI is therefore not a mere economic battle but has far-reaching geopolitical dimensions. India's withdrawal is being perceived as a betrayal under US pressure, which arguably may not be the case as India has her own apprehensions about the project. A little more on it, in subsequent section.

IP and TAPI are therefore manifestation of a New Great Game being played between various powers basically to control the Oil and Natural Gas assets of the region, to bring the nuclear aspirant Iran to heals besides breaking the stranglehold of Russia on the resources of Central Asian Region and do not allow Pakistan to tread a policy independent of US under the regional cooperative mechanism. At another level it can be considered a tug of war between Gazprom and CNPC on one side and Chevron, Exxon Mobil and Arco and many other Oil and Gas Multinational giants on the other side which is being fronted by Russia, Chinese on one side and USA on the other side. Losers in any scenario are going to be Iran and Pakistan mainly and India generally. While it is true that a number of factors are being resulting into the course of action which is getting unfolded however which is that one driver which is the catalyst of the evolving scenario is difficult to identify. It seems that it is the geo-political interests of different stake holders are the main drivers. US' 'concerns' with regard to this project have geo-political underpinnings and explain its opposition to IP pipeline. Geo-political importance of Pakistan and Iran, under current regional circumstances, for the US as well as India can be appreciated, when internal and external dynamics of the polities of both Pakistan and Iran is taken into account. Also the locational advantage of both these countries in the context of control of land routes from Central Asia as well as shipping in the Persian Gulf and the Strait of Hormuz make these countries an object of great interest to all stake holders *(Interpretation and analysis of the author, based on the inputs from Huzaima Bukhari and Dr Ikramul Haq (member Taxand) and Adjunct Professors at Lahore University of Management Sciences (LUMS), 'The news' of Pakistan and The International Tribune)*

Section-7: International Gas Pipelines

One of the options to import natural gas, which the Indian government has been examining for a while, now; is to use transnational gas pipelines. Many of these have not proved to be feasible. In 2005, negotiations between the Indian and Bangladesh governments fell through over a transnational pipeline. In 2006, India left the Iran-Pakistan-India (IPI) pipeline project. One pipeline which still looks feasible is the one which originates in Turkmenistan. In this project, the government of India is still participating in the discussions and is hopeful for it to become operational.

The Turkmenistan-Afghanistan-Pakistan-India (TAPI) project-

The idea was conceived in 1990, around 1790 Kms in length and origin adjacent to Caspian Sea. Collapse of Soviet Union was the major catalyst in its getting conceptualised. The Basic document for the promotion of the TAPI gas pipeline project is the 'Ashgabad Interstate Agreement of the State Parties on the commencement of the practical implementation of the TAPI Project signed in late 2010.

It will be 48 inch diameter pipeline having the designed capacity of the TAPI pipeline is 33 BCM of Natural Gas/ year and it will supply 90 MCM of gas per day from Turkmenistan to participating nations with the distribution of 38 MCM per day each to India and Pakistan and 14 MCM per day to Afghanistan .

The estimated length reaches 1735 Kms at the Indo-Pak Border. Of TAPI's total 1,680 Kms up to Indo Pak Border, 144 Kms will be in Turkmenistan, 735 Kms in Afghanistan, and 800 Kms in Pakistan. The origin of the pipeline would be in Turkmenistan's Galkynysh (previously South Yolotan Osman and also known as Dauletabad) field. From there it will be up to Guspi (Turkmenistan), through Herat, Lashkargah, and Kandahar (Afghanistan), and Quetta, GG Khan, Multan, and Pakpattan (Pakistan), to its end at the Indian border town of Fazilka (Fig. 7.1).

GAIL will buy the Indian portion of gas and will have the option of being part of the consortium building the pipeline. With proven gas reserves of 16 TCM, Galkynysh would produce 411.173 BCM/year of gas over 30 years. (Pak News Service). On June 7, 2012, Reliance Industries Ltd (RIL), India's petrochemical giant, said it intends to source a sustained 60 MMCMD of additional gas supply in the next 3-4 years with the help of quick government and regulatory approvals. This timing coincides roughly with TAPI participants' targeted October 2017 in-service date. (Tridivesh Singh Maini and Manish Vaid)

Figure-7.1

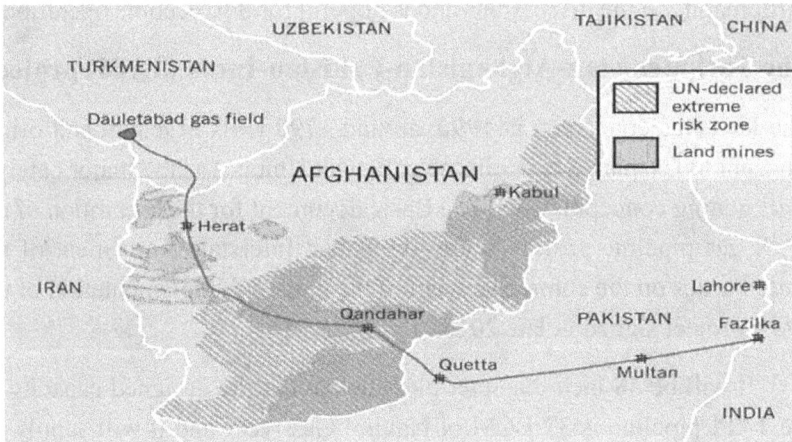

Though the estimated cost is $ 7.6 billion, the Asian Development Bank estimates the cost of the pipeline would reach about $10-12 billion. The stake holders have made some progress in moving TAPI forward in recent times. The partners signed a framework agreement in 2010 and agreed on unified transit tariffs for the route in early 2012. In May 2012, India signed gas supply and purchase agreement with Turkmenistan. In early February 2013, India's government approved a special purpose vehicle (SPV) to which participating members of the pipeline would contribute investment funds with a view to carry out pre project activities and to finalize an appropriate consortium leader for the Project. The initial equity contribution of India in the proposed SPV (TAPI Ltd.) would be $ 5 million.

Further investments would be negotiated and decided upon the induction of Consortium Leader and after completion of the Feasibility Study. Commercial operation of TAPI Pipeline Project is expected to commence in 2017-18. (Parliament proceedings) It appears that the thought process is to get the project executed by an International Company. It has emerged that most of the companies want a part of gas equity as a condition for bidding for the project, basically to safeguard their interests in view of the imponderables associated with the project due to a volatile security situation as well as an envisaged likely fickle nature of the response of the Turkmenistan Government. So far the government of Turkmenistan does not agree to this condition as their law does not permit. However negotiations are on to resolve the issue. (Discussion with the officials of MoP & NG and MEA)

Analysis of the Project

- It has the backing of USA who wants to support it for two reasons. Firstly to see to it that IPI does not fructify and Iran is economically pressurised and secondly to break the strangle hold of Russia on the resources of Central Asian Countries.

- Necessary tie ups complete.

- All stake holders namely Turkmenistan, Afghanistan, Pakistan and India are keen for it to fructify based on their respective national interests.

- Weakness is that the agency which is going to execute it, has not yet been identified.

- It will contribute to the energy kitty of Pakistan and India which will partially bridge the yawning gap of the energy existing/ impending deficit in their respective countries. It will be more beneficial to Pakistan as Pakistan has no option but to go for pipeline (No LNG terminal as yet) and IPI's future quite uncertain. This pipeline will help Pakistan to bridge a shortfall of gas supply by one billion units per day in shortest possible time frame. Even for Afghanistan it offers a great opportunity. Though Afghanistan does not want gas but $ 300 million as transit fee is a substantial incentive. In fact Afghanistan is likely to get 8 percent of the revenue generated by the TAPI and a fair share of job opportunities (Including personnel for the security of the pipeline) generated. (Daly J). No wonder both the countries have committed that the physical safety of the pipeline would be assured. For Turkmenistan it is an opportunity to earn revenue for the well sought resource that they have in plenty and also diversify into a big market like South Asia. (Mahapatra, DA) Economic interdependence between Pakistan-Afghanistan and India-Pakistan and is going to help to improve their bilateral relations. Increased supplies of pipeline gas will also help India and Pakistan to diversify their energy trade and industrial bases (Vaid M). India has offered to build a pipeline to the Wagah border to ship 50 million tons per year of petroleum products, with lower transportation costs allowing delivery at prices 30 percent below what Pakistan currently pays (Press Trust of India). The fall in Pakistan's natural gas production since 2010 has prompted it to ask India for immediate heating oil imports (Jayaswal R).

- It will pass through some of the most volatile regions in the world more so post US withdrawal from Afghanistan in 2014; physical safety would be a major issue. Especially its passage through Pakistan makes India not very comfortable. But in this regard it needs to be understood that the success of this pipeline is a greater necessity of Pakistan than India. More over historically even at the height of Cold War Russia never stopped gas supply to Western Europe (Russia has stopped gas /oil only twice once in 2006 and second time in 2009 basically to teach a lesson to Ukraine who they alleged were stealing resources meant for Western Europe). Another example is that of Baku-Tbilisi-Ceyhan (BTC) pipeline which passes through equally volatile region but has been successful. (Khadim Shahid)

- Recently it has been reported that Turkmenistan has diversified in supply of gas to China and Iran, but it has been confirmed by the Minister of Economy and Development of Turkmenistan that those agreements with China and Iran will not affect the quantity of gas meant for TAPI. (Statement of Turkmen Minister of Economy and Development at World Economic Forum).

Iran-Pakistan-India Pipeline

Iran has a gas reserve of 27.8 TCM which makes it second largest stock holder after Russia. The Iran-Pakistan-India (IPI) Pipeline has been under discussion since 1994. The plan calls for a 2700 Kms long land based 42 inch pipeline starting from South Pars gas field in Persian Gulf, Iran to Delhi via Karachi and Multan in Pakistan. First 1100 Kms will be in Iran, next 1000 Kms in Pakistan and last 600 Kms in India.

Figure-7.2

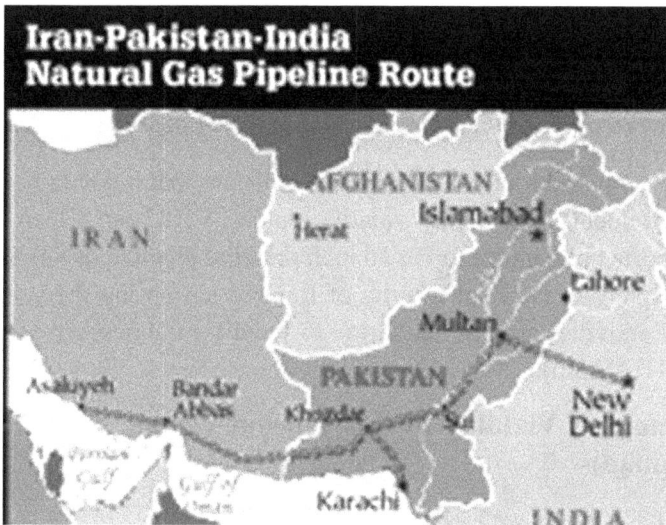

Its full developmental cost is likely to be in excess of $ 7 billion with a capacity of 5.4 BCFD. Besides gas Pakistan will also earn a yearly transit fee of $200-$500 million. Pipeline will carry 110 MCM of gas per day and 50 MCM of it will be consumed by Iran and balance 60 MCM will be delivered to Pakistan. If project goes through India will get 50 percent of the 22 BCM and balance will be retained by Pakistan. The MoU was signed between Iran and Pakistan in May 2009 and the project was signed in May 2010. On 02 Feb 2013 the foundation stone was jointly laid President Asif Ali Zardari of Pakistan and President Mahmaud Ahmadinejad of Iran. (Gulf Oil Gas Com) As per that Iran will supply 750 MCFD for 25 years. Iran has already completed its portion and it is expected that the pipeline (Iran-Pakistan) will ready by 2014. Iran is also taking up the construction of the portion in Pakistan. The cost of gas is estimated to be $7.2/ MBTU.

At the point of delivery India will pay an additional sum of $1.1-$1.2/ MBTU towards the transportation cost and transit fee and that will make it one of the costliest gas.

To reduce the cost the Iranian government filed a request with the Pakistani government for extension of the proposed gas pipeline to India. For Pakistan, the extension was acceptable to Pakistan, but it took India more than a decade to digest the idea of gas transmission over the territory of Pakistan, with which it has had various armed conflicts and an as of yet unresolved dispute over the area of Kashmir. India does not feel entirely comfortable with the idea of being dependent in the long run on Pakistan. Thus even though there is an acute shortage of energy and especially natural gas in India, the Indian government is still not enthusiastic about entering into an agreement with Pakistan regarding gas transit. (Case Study, by International Gas Union's Gas market Integration Task Forces).

The proposed route of the pipeline indicates that it would be passing through Baluchistan a highly volatile region of Pakistan which had six cases reported of damage to the 16 inch pressure pipeline of Sui Southern Gas Company in Jafrabad District of Baluchistan during the year 2010-11. Such activities are not reassuring to India for the passage of the gas. (Shabbir H Kazmi).

Assessment of Viability of this Pipeline (inputs from Aziz-ud-Din-Ahmad)-

- Pakistan as well as Iran have very high stakes in the successful completion of the pipeline; Iran to earn revenue which post US sanctions are drying up and Pakistan because, as has been established earlier, it needs energy to sustain its economy. Pak feels that as against TAPI it has a better chance to get completed earlier.

- USA/ UN sanctions are big hurdles because they are affecting the economy/ access to technology. India which is bound by the UN economic sanctions, security situation and the cost of the gas is not very keen to be part of the project and it needs to be understood clearly that without Indian participation, chances of it becoming a reality are not very bright.

- Saudi Arabia is also keen that this pipeline does not come through basically with a view to contain Iran.

- While most political parties in Pakistan have their vested interests and making right noise without openly expressing against it, are not making efforts for it to go through for their respective reasons.

- Militants in Baluchistan in any case are a big threat to survivability of the pipeline. It also needs to be noted that militant Sunni lobby in Pakistan does not want it to succeed as it would benefit Shia Iran.

Variety of economic, political and security issues have delayed a project agreement. Due to the uncertainties involving this pipeline, the Government of India since 11th Five Year Plan has not been factoring any gas supply from this pipeline. India thus began looking at yet another alternative means of attaining Iranian gas, through an offshore pipeline which would skirt Pakistani territory altogether. But after a detailed field study offshore route was not found to be feasible.

Imports from Myanmar

The OVL and GAIL bought 20 per cent and 10 per cent stake respectively, in A1 and A3 blocks in Myanmar off shore gas field off Sittwe. Together these blocks have proven gas reserves of about 4.5 TCF. The governments of India and Myanmar signed a natural gas supply deal in 2006, but disagreement arose over the route particularly whether the pipeline should pass through Bangladesh or not. This project, envisaged as an important aspect of the energy security policy of India, has in the past failed to accommodate the needs of Bangladesh; this has resulted in an indefinite delay in project implementation. As an alternative the project was planned to pass through the North-Eastern Region (NER). Inordinate delay in finalising the project route resulted into Myanmar deciding to sell all the gas to China, delivering a deadly blow to India's ambitious project. In March 2009, Myanmar signed a natural gas supply deal with China to transport 12 MMT of Crude Oil and 12 BCM of Gas per year to Yunnan in China, sourced from this oil/gas field. Myanmar-China pipeline project consists of dual oil and gas pipelines originate at Kyaukryu port on the west coast of Myanmar and enter China at Yunnan's border city of Ruili. (Vargonda Kesava Chandra). The natural gas reserves in Myanmar are limited – and at this stage Myanmar is not in a position to accommodate the needs of both China and the Indo-Bangladesh partnership. According to the Production Sharing Contract (PSC), ONGC Videsh Limited (OVL) and Gas Authority of India Limited (GAIL) had the right to sell domestically or export their share of about 2 MMSCMD gas to China. The Indo-Myanmar gas pipeline project is finally off as confirmed by the Minister of Petroleum in Jul 2009, as an economically unviable project. (Assam tribune) The lack of convergence in the energy security policies of India and Bangladesh has impacted the outcome of the Myanmar-Bangladesh-India (MBI) pipeline project. However, recent changes in the energy scenario of Bangladesh have enabled greater convergence in the energy policies of both countries leading once again to prospects of a revival of the project. But probably it is a case of being 'too late'. No longer gas from this pipeline is being taken into account while planning the energy supply by the Indian planners. Although it may not be very significant quantitatively but accretion of this gas would have contributed substantially for the development of NER and as such would have addressed an important aspect of national security.

Figure-7.3

Route of Proposed Myanmar-India Gas Pipeline

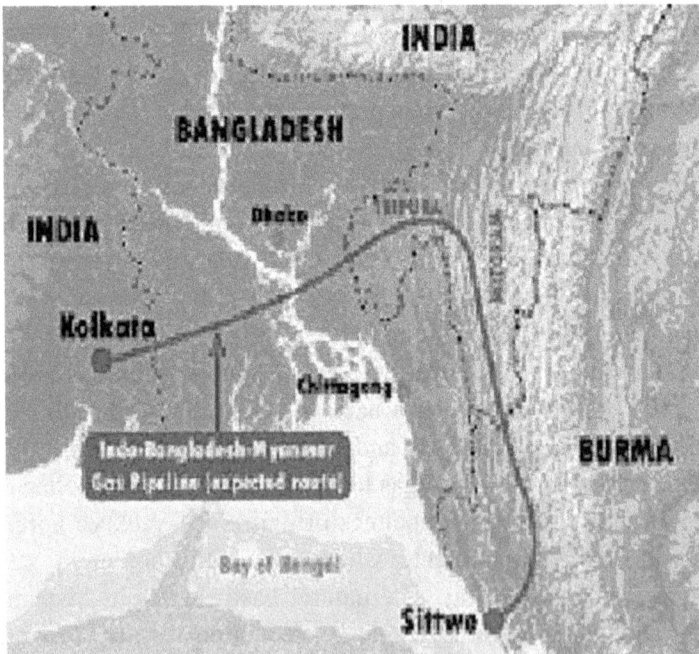

Section-8: Liquefied Natural Gas (LNG) - A Game Changer

LNG Process- Natural gas is chilled to minus 160°C to create a colourless liquid 1/600th of its original volume for long distance shipment aboard tankers. At destination the liquid gas is again re-gasified in the LNG Terminal for further transportation to its destination of utilisation. The cost of establishing a LNG terminal is quite substantial. A rough indicator is that the fixed cost is $10 billion besides the cost of the pipeline from/ to terminal, cost of transportation tankers and the cost of refrigeration plant.

LNG: A Way Ahead- The world demand is going to become more than double by 2035. In real terms it would be to the tune of 6.6 TCM a year. The global demand is likely to outpace LNG supplies around the end of this decade and may exceed production by 100 MMT (4.87 TCM) annually by 2025. (John Swatsus). In USA 19 projects are awaiting export permit. On the other hand Canada has already created a capacity to ship 4.66 billion cubic feet (BCF) of gas/ day (Joe Carrol and Rebecca Penty).

LNG in India's Energy Matrix- It has become an important part of India's energy mix. India started LNG import in 2004 when for the first time LNG import contract was signed with RAS Gas of Qatar. India has increasingly been relying on imported LNG. It became the sixth largest LNG importer in 2011 with 5.3% of global imports (In 2011-2012 the total import has reached 10.13 MMTPA) (PPAC Data), according to data from PFC energy. Indian companies have begun investing in new re-gasification facilities to meet rising demand. Indian companies use both long-term supply contracts and more expensive spot LNG contracts. Indian companies have also been attempting to secure new longer-term deals with suppliers such as Russia's Gazprom. The Petronet, a joint venture between GAIL, ONGC, and several foreign firms, is the major importer of LNG supplies to India. Petronet owns the country's two currently operational LNG terminals, Dahej and Hazira, and plans to increase capacity of both these plants. Unexpected production decline in India's KG D-6 gas field has triggered higher LNG imports. Imported LNG is typically more than twice as expensive as domestically produced natural gas, because it is not subject to the government setting prices through the Administered Price Mechanism. Presently, (2011 estimates) there are 18 countries exporting the gas and 28 countries are importing the LNG. The prevailing rates are $ 3 per MMBTU for USA, in Europe the price is $ 11-13 per MMBTU and in South East Asia it is as high as $ 18 per MMBTU. The spot market of the Gas has not yet developed as is the case with the Crude Oil. There are two types of rates. First is called Henry Hub prices. These are valid only for countries with which USA has a FTA Agreement. The other internationally common system is; Japanese Custom Cleared Crude (JCCC), popularly known as the Japanese Crude Cocktail prices. The price difference between the two prices is quite substantial (US $2-4 as Henry Hub rate and US $ 12-14 for Japanese Cocktail). Such high prices are, in fact, a bad news for India, because; by 2025 India will be biggest gas importer country. As a part of the Government's policy a number of LNG terminals are coming up (Sec 14.183, draft 12th Plan Document). According to India's Oil and Natural Gas Ministry, the Petronet's LNG terminal at Kochi is likely to become operational in 2013, itself. GAIL and NTPC along with and several other smaller players have already restarted the Dabhol project. As far as India's east coast is concerned, IOC has proposed a project in Tamil Nadu (Ennore). Other possible projects include a floating terminal at Kakinada as a substitute for declining gas production in the Krishna-Godavari basin. Qatar's Ras Gas is India's sole long-term supplier of natural gas, with two contracts for a total of 360 billion cubic feet (BCF). India has been an active spot importer and has been receiving LNG cargoes from a variety of exporting countries. In recent times, Nigeria and Egypt have risen in prominence as India's short-term suppliers.

LNG Infrastructure in the Country

Table-8.1

Existing LNG Terminals in India

RGPL LNG Terminal at Dabhol Maharashtra	5 MMTPA
Dahej Terminal, PETRONET LNG Ltd, Gujarat	10 MMTPA
Hazira Terminal, Shell Ltd, Gujarat	3.5 MMTPA
Kochi, PETRONET LNG, Kerala	5 MMTPA

New LNG Terminals- Six new LNG terminals are coming up at; RGPPL Dabhol, Petronet Kochi, GSPC Pipavav, GSPC Mundra, ONGC Mangalore (all on Western Coast) and IOCL Ennore (on Eastern Coast). Out of these Dhabol and Mundra have capacities of 5 MMTPA. (Marubeni. com & business-standard.com). Pipavav and Managalore will have initial capacity of 2.5 MMTPA, extendable to 5 MMTPA. Kochi *abinitio* will have a capacity of 5 MMTPA. All of these will be ready in a staggered timeframe by 2018. (Money control.com, Et Bureau and Wikipedia).

Impact of US Shale Gas on the Natural Gas/ LNG Market in the World

With the new breakthrough in the Shale gas exploration, the USA has become net exporter of gas with effect from December 2011 (refer Figure-8.1). Besides advent of Shale Gas other factors like improved refining capacity, reduced demand also contributed to this status. Herein lies a lesson for India to; not only enhance supply of desired form of the energy by various means but also find/ innovate/ institutionalise ways and means to improve demand side management with a view to reduce the demand itself and as such shorten the gap between the demand and the supply.

Figure- 8.1

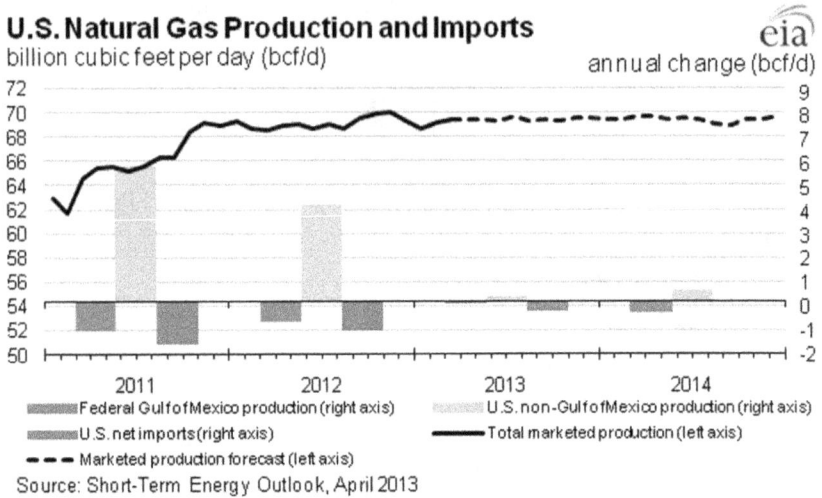

Source: Short-Term Energy Outlook, April 2013

Though presently USA has only one LNG export terminal but other 18 existing import terminals are being proposed to be converted to export terminals. The export of the gas from the USA is controlled by Department of the Energy (DOE) of the USA as per the Section II of the National Gas Act of 1938. The countries with which the USA has a FTA get the gas at Henry Hub rates. The non FTA partners can be reviewed on a case to case basis provided they meet a national interest test (Gary Clyde Huf Bauer, Alice E Bagnali and Julia Muir).

Status of Gas Trade with US and Other Countries: Options and Recommendations-

- Presently there is no plan to grant India a FTA status. However a one-time waiver has been given to GAIL to import 3.5 Million Tons Per Annum (MTPA) on a free-on-board (FOB) basis for 20 years from Cheniere Energy beginning in 2017, linked to Henry Hub prices (Nidhi Verma and Jo Winterbottom).

- There is need to either through acquisitions or through waiver route to get more LNG from USA at FTA rates to compensate for the loss of options of gas through IPI pipe line which, due to sanctions on Iran is unlikely to come through.

- An assessment will also reveal that with US demand for import getting reduced is resulting into Australian, Indonesian, Canadian and Omanis' gas becoming surplus in the market and as such available. Individual agreements can be considered with these countries.

- GAIL and Reliance are also going for a number of acquisitions in USA for the gas/ Shell gas to enhance the availability of the cheaper gas.

- With a number of new LNG terminals being planned in 12th Plan and an emphasis on construction of a number of offshore supply vessels it appears that India is attempting to live without the gas from IPI and also not waiting for TAPI to fructify. In any case the quantum of gas from both IPI and TAPI will not be adequate to meet the yawning gap between demand and supply. Hence alternate routes/ technologies/ business models will have to found and necessary infrastructure will have to be built accordingly.

Section-9: Way Ahead

The analysis of various issues having bearing on Energy/ Energy Security in previous sections of the paper clearly brings out hat Pakistan is definitely important for the energy security of India, if India wants to have a lien on the gas from Central Asia as well as Iran. However even in the most optimistic scenario flow of gas is not likely in next five years. Therefore alternatives will have to be found to cater for period in next few years (up to 2017-18). One of the discovery (Shale Gas) and development of its commercial exploitation by leveraging technology by the USA has changed the world energy scene substantially. Plenty of LNG which earlier was going to USA is now available in the market and can be procured after due negotiations. In this connection an engagement with USA, who, itself has now become net exporter, needs to be initiated. As far as these pipelines are concerned, efforts on these should not be allowed to get dampened because their becoming operational will facilitate greater economic integration of India-Pakistan and also India Bangladesh. It will also enhance greater economic interdependence between the stake holders and as such would contribute towards national security.

An appraisal of the 12th Plan Document read in conjunction with Hydro carbon Vision-2025, Integrated Energy Policy, discussions with the concerned officials in the Government of India and Think Tanks have brought certain aspects which merit consideration. Those issues and recommended action with respect to those areas are as elaborated in subsequent paragraphs.

Research and Development In Newer Resources-

- **Shale Gas-**

    - It is increasingly becoming the fuel of tomorrow. However presently there is no comprehensive policy existing. It was confirmed by the concerned officials in the Ministry of Petroleum and Natural Gas that the policy formulation is in the final stage- it needs to be expedited.

- **Shale Gas Exploration**- Government has initiated steps for development of shale oil and shale gas from on land sedimentary basins. A MoU has been signed between Ministry of Petroleum & Natural Gas and Department of State, USA on 6 December 2010 for cooperation in resource assessment, regulatory framework, training and so on. A multi-organisation team (MOT) has been constituted involving DGH, ONGC, OIL and GAIL for collection of required G & G, geochemical and petro-physical data for assessment of shale oil and shale gas prospects in Indian on land sedimentary basins. The involvement of private sector in this initiative will be enhanced as well. A policy of regulatory framework is to be put in place for shale oil and shale gas development- policy is still under formulation (Sec 14.177 of Plan document).

- Acquisition of shale bearing properties abroad and exploration within the country needs to be expedited.

- In this connection certain aspects about the state of Shale gas in India need to be given a serious consideration before a decision with respect to planning the incorporation of Indian Shale Gas in the energy security matrix is taken. These issues are mentioned in succeeding sub-sub paragraphs.

- Indian shales are not believed to be as prolific as those which are there in USA, China or Europe. The problem, understood so far, with the Indian shales is the permeability characteristic which is quite different from the US shales. The current fracking technologies are designed for rigid and brittle shales, rich in organic material and therefore enough gas. On the other hand Indian shales may be younger and are more likely to be soft and ductile in comparison to these shales. (Sunjoy Joshi, A The Times of India Report dated 04 May 2013)

- In India the Shale bearing strata is located in areas having very high density of population and land presently being used for agriculture. Whether the land would at all be available for exploration is another issue which needs deliberation

- Its exploration is taken an aspect which needs a very serious consideration is the utilisation of water whose large quantities would be needed for hydraulic fracturing to extract Shale Gas (2,500,000 CUM per year). This contaminated water is likely to pollute the ground water with adverse environment impact (Arthur, J. Daniel; Uretsky, Mike; Wilson, Preston). Whether water stressed country like India can afford it or not? This issue needs serious examination.

- **National Gas Hydrate Programme (NGHP)-** As an unconventional hydrocarbon resource, methane hydrates have been the focus of India's quest for meeting her energy demands and it was with this objective that India's National Gas Hydrate Program(NGHP) was launched by Ministry of Petroleum and Natural Gas . Steered by the MoP&NG and technically coordinated by the Directorate General Of Hydrocarbons (DGH), NGHP is a consortium of National E&P companies (ONGC and GAIL) and National Research Institutions (National Institute of Oceanography, National Geophysical Research Institute and National Institute of Ocean Technology). (Directorate General of Hydrocarbons Communiqué) As per the Road Map (Oil Industry Development Board Communiqué) the commercial production of methane from gas hydrates is still a farfetched thought although NGHP has set itself a deadline of mid 2015 as the time to commence commercial production, the commercial production of methane from Indian Gas Hydrate resources has its own set of challenges, a few would perhaps be as follows:-

    - Absence of representative deepwater gas hydrates field anywhere in the world

    - Gas production rate (Gas in the production testing of Mallik well in Canada's permafrost area have yielded very low production rate and could not sustain more than 7 days of production using thermal and depressurization methods)

- Managing Water production rate (High amount of water is expected to be produced along with the dissociation of hydrates)

- Sand control since the hydrate reservoirs exist at very shallow depth below sea bed (200-400 mbsf) the sands here would not be consolidated due to absence of overburden pressure.

- Reservoir subsidence and other environmental hazards

- These challenges can only be overcome by sustained commitment of our scientists and establishment of a proper gas hydrate R&D center in India. The global gas hydrate communities of scientists and researchers have to work in tandem with each other. DGH on behalf of the NGHP has signed Memoranda of Understanding in the field of Gas Hydrates with Japan Oil, Gas, Metal Corporation JOGMEC, Gas Hydrate R&D Organisation (GHDO) of the Korea Institute of Geology, Mining and Materials (KIGAM) and the US Department of Energy (USDOE) another MOU with the US Geological Survey (USGS) is in the pipeline. DGH has been closely associated with the USGS , USDOE and JOGMEC scientists which has helped the NGHP scientists to gain a lot in terms of knowledge, understanding and experience. a MoU was recently signed in the area of marine gas hydrate research and technology development between the Leibniz Institute of Marine Sciences, Germany and DGH for research on methane production from gas hydrate by carbon dioxide sequestration. Efforts need to intensify to take programme to logical conclusion at the earliest. (Sec 14.179 of the Plan Document).

- Newer areas identified for further progress by Planning Commission during 12th Plan are; coal bed methane, gas hydrate, shale gas, oil shale etc. Oil companies also need to focus on development of renewable energy sources including biodiesel, ethanol, wind, solar, biomass and so on to make the hydrocarbon use for various activities carbon neutral by the companies (Sec 14.174 of the Plan document).

- **Wind Power-** India is the second largest wind turbine manufacturer next to China. The installed manufacturing capacity in India ranges around 6,000 MW per year of turbine more than 2 MW capacities. In recent times Capacity Utilisation Factor (CUF) has gone up from 10-12% in 1998 to 22% in 2012. Next step in technology up-gradation in areas of aerodynamic design, other aspects of material, component design and installation height to exploit greater intensity of wind. Wind energy needs to be concentrated on to augment the energy availability. (Sec 14.211 and 14.212 of Plan Document.

Conceptual Framework- It is important to realise that the conceptual framework to attain the energy security will be different for different countries. Because solutions based on non indigenous resources may give rise to problems of environment and may not be conducive for sustained growth, in the absence of uninterrupted supply assurance. Therefore the strategy should be based on minimum import dependency, optimum utilisation of local resources and enough redundancy based on multi sourcing.

Recommendations with respect to Energy market- There are six main challenges that need to be addressed to create a well-functioning and financially-viable energy market in India:-

- The core capacities of players in India's energy sector – mainly, energy companies – should be improved. Energy players need to be commercially viable, with access to adequate financial resources.

- Pricing mechanisms in the energy sector must ensure commercial viability and send proper signals to the market. The current rigid pricing setting mechanism, which is de facto determined by the government, should be reformed. Sector regulators should be enabled to operate independently from political influence. End-use pricing should support the government's policy for demand-side management and facilitate a rational allocation of resources along the value-chain.

- India requires significant investment to meet its growing energy demand and provide access to all citizens, many of which are excluded from access to modern and clean sources of energy. Investment in the energy sector should focus on adopting the latest, green growth.

- An increase in effective implementation of energy policies is required through the improvement of bureaucratic and administrative processes to assure a timely completion of energy projects.

- Truly integrated and consistent energy policy is critical to guide and direct India's energy sector and ensure investment. Pursuing multiple policy objectives through one energy policy can potentially undermine the actual achievement of energy policy objectives.

- Strong political will is a prerequisite to successfully cope with energy sector challenges. India should complete the unfinished reforms on its energy sector based on market-principles.

Evolution of a Framework for an Effective Energy Management- In India the energy management is an extremely complex activity because organisationally a large number of departments and at least five/eight ministries (five energy/power ministries plus MEA, which contributes at diplomatic level for import of energy bearing resources, DST for import/cooperation in the field of technology infusion and ministry of commerce to enhance interdependence) in a two level system work, many a times independent of each other. Also the field of technology is fast changing and the new inventions/ evolutions/ innovations are opening up new areas for improving both supply side as well as demand side management. Another issue typical to India is the mismatch between the indigenous resources and the technologies available locally for their optimum exploitation to bridge the gap between demand and supply. Here a coordinated approach with industry will be required to meet the challenges of availability, cost consideration, need and efforts to evolve technologies to exploit resources locally available and finally locational imbalances. For an energy deficient India a strong R&D well supported by the government as well as the industry is needed to continuously evolve new commercially viable technologies to meet future challenges using local resources. This presently is not very effective. One of the important reasons is a lack of coordination between academia, industry and the decision maker. Next weakness; which affects the energy supply is the lack of coordination among various departments dealing with the subject. In fact effort of each department is independent of others. This brings out the need for a strong over arching organisation for coordination. Therefore to cater for provision of adequate energy in a sustained manner at affordable cost, need for following elements as a part of an energy management system need to be considered for efficient management of move of energy from pithead/source to switch board:-

- A central Agency for coordination and planning- presently this task is being done by the Planning Commission. It needs to have a better forecasting arrangement and should be empowered. Besides policy directions which should be able to respond to changing technological development, geopolitical/ geo-economic scenarios. It should also have capability built into its organisation to provide ways and means for capacity building both of HR and also of industry at policy level.

- Organisation of Funding for the energy utilisation.

- Risk Mitigation arrangements are formalised and reviewed from time to time to respond to new emerging situations.

- **Supply Side Management**- aim would be increase the supply to optimum level.

    - Improving the capacity of R&D in conjunction with Industry with respect to indigenous resources for which economically viable technology is not available.

    - Improving storage arrangement as per policy to cater for disruptions and logistic arrangement to transfer the stored asset to the place of use.

    - Enhancing grid connectivity across the country and its monitoring mechanism for implementation.

    - Enhancing the energy supply from the all available resources by finding ways and means to optimise their output. It could be area specific and the surplus/ deficiency be addressed through comprehensive, efficient and effective grid system..

- Arrangements in consultation with the MEA to facilitate import of those resources for which technology is available. Simultaneously Infrastructure built up to receive those resources and move them to place of conversion be thought of. In consultation with commerce ministry these imports could be used to create interdependence to sustain those imports.

- Diplomacy is used to tackle restrictive regimes.

- **Demand Side Management**- aim would to reduce the demand by using measures some of the important ones are as follows:-

  - Conservation- by having better norms for building and standardisation of equipment.

  - Improve efficiency of equipment from exploration to switch board.

  - Plantation to reduce the need for excessive air conditioning.

  - Rain water harvesting to raise the water table to reduce energy needs for pumping.

The measures listed are neither fully comprehensive nor final. A lot of deliberation further needs to be done to examine all aspects of the system envisaged and also experiences of many of the developed countries who are managing their resources optimally, need to be studied to incorporate them into the system which needs to be evolved so that the system that emerges, responds to the constantly evolving/ changing felt needs of the environment in all possible contingencies.

References and Bibliography

Annual report of the State Bank of Pakistan: 2011-12.

A 'Daily Times' Report, "Pakistan consumes half of its Gas reserves" dated 28 Dec 2011, uploaded on www.dailytimes.com.pk/default.asp?page=2011%5C12%5C28%5CStory_28-12-2011_pg5_10

Arthur, J. Daniel; Uretsky, Mike; Wilson, Preston (May 5–6, 2010). "Water Resources and Use for Hydraulic Fracturing in the Marcellus Shale Region" (PDF). Meeting of the American Institute of Professional Geologists.Pittsburgh: ALL Consulting. p. 3. Retrieved 2012-05-09.

Arvind Jayaram, BL Research, "Dependence on Crude Oil Imports on the Rise", The Hindu Business Line, dated 19 Jul 2012.

As told by Dr Sarbinder Singh , SARI-Energy during an Interview with David Temple, 20 October 2006.

Special Correspondent, Assam Tribune,"Indo-Myanmar gas pipeline project shelved", Pub in Assam Tribune, 30 Jul 2009.

Asma Shakir Khwaja, " Pakistan and the 'New Great game'", IPRI paper 5 Apr 2003 uploaded on ipripak.org/papers/pakandnewgame.shtml.

Aziz-ud-Din-Ahmad, "Will Iran Pakistan Gas pipeline Survive", pub in Pakistan Today, 15 Mar 2013, uploaded on www.pakistantoday.com.pk/2013/03/15/comments/columns/will-iran-pakistan-gas-pipeline-survive/

BBC News, "US Approves Indian Nuclear Deal", 09 Dec 2006.

Behrooz Esrafili-Dizaji and Hossain Rahimpour-Bonab, University of Tehran, "Iranian Discoveries continue" pub in E& P Magazine of)01 Apr 2012, uploaded on http;//www.epmamag.com/item/Iranian-discoveries-continue-98522

Behrooz Esrafili-Dizaji, Farkhondeh Kiani Harchegani, University of Tehran, "Persia Land of Black Gold", published in GEO Expro, Issue2, Volume10, 2013, uploaded on www.geoexpro.com/article_Land_of_Black_Gold/e7e95f74.aspx

BS Reporters, "OVL-OIL Offers $5 bn for 20% in Africa gas field", pub in Business Standard, dated01 April 2013, uploaded on www.business-standard.com/article/companies/ovl-oil-5-bn-for-20-in-africa-gas-field-113033100202_1.html

Country Analysis Brief: Turkmenistan by Energy Information Administration of USA updated up to Dec 2012, uploaded on http://www.eia.gov/cabs/Turkmenistan/pdf.pdf and retreived on 06 May 2013

Daly J, "On Again, Off Again Trans-Afghan Natural Gas Pipeline Revives", pub in Oil Price, 30 Jan 2012

David Temple, "The Iran-Pakistan-India Pipeline, The Intersection of Energy and Politics", pub by Institute of Peace and Conflict Studies, New Delhi, India.

Directorate General of Hydrocarbons (under Ministry of Petroleum and Natural Gas), uploaded on www.dgh.dghindia.org/NonconventionalEnergy.aspx?tab=0

Discussion with the officials of the Ministry of the Petroleum and the Natural Gas, Government of India on 09 April 2013 and JS Energy security in MEA.

Draft of the 12th Plan Document.

Energy Security Handbook, pub by Energy Security division of MEA, Government of India.

ET Bureau, "Gujrat Plans LNG Terminal at Pipavav Port", pub in Economic Times dated 30 Mar 2013.

Farooq Tirmizi,"The Myth of Pakistan's InfiniteGas Reserves", published in 'The express Tribune' dated 14 jan 2011

Gary Clyde Huf Bauer, Alice E Bagnali and Julia Muir: Policy Brief," Liquefied Natural Gas Exports: An Opportunity for America", pub in

Peterson Institute of International economics, Number PB13-6 dated Feb 2013.

Guy F. Caruso and Linda E. Doman, "Global Energy Supplier and the U.S. Market," Economic Perspectives, May 2004.

Huzaima Bukhari and Dr Ikramul Haq, " IPI Vs TAPI- Great War of Interests", dated 14 Jan 2012, uploaded on www. uzaimaikram. worldpress.com/category/politics/page/2/

Huzaima Bukhari and Dr Ikramul Haq, "The Great Game" published in 'The News' and uploaded on jang.com.pk/thenews/mar2013-weekly/ nos-17-03-2013/pol1.htm#4

Index Mundi, "Pakistan Economy Profile 2013", with inputs from CIA World Fact Book: info as on Feb 2013, uploaded on www.indexmundi. com/pakistan/economy_profile.html and retrieved on 04 May 2013

India Hydrocarbon Vision-2025, Pub by Ministry of P&NG, Government of India.

Jayaswal, R., "Pakistan Is Willing to Import Furnace Oil, Diesel, and Natural Gas from India," The Economic Times, July 18, 2012.

Joe Carroll and Rebecca Penty, " Canada Seen Beating US in $ 150 billion on Asia LNG Race", reported by Bloomberg dated 04 April 2013 and uploaded on www.bloomberg.com/news/2013-04-02/canada-seen-beating-u-s-in-150billion-asia-lng-race.html

John Swatsus to analysts in New York during Mar 2013.

Khadim Shahid, "Pipeline Deje vu," pub in International The News, Apr 12, 2013. Also published in Oriental Review: Org SA Global Affairs, Uploaded on orientalreview.org/2013/04/01/us-policy-towards-iran-pakistan-gas-pipeline-i/

Mehdi Parvizi Amineh and Henk Houweling, "Caspian Energy: Oil and Gas Resources and the Global Market," in Mehdi Parvizi Amineh and Henk Houweling, ed-, Central Eurasia in Global Politics: Conflict, Security and Development (Koninklijke Brill NV: Leiden, the Netherlands, 2005), 77-78.

Ministry of Power, Government of India, uploaded on official website of the ministry: http://powermin.nic.in/h

Mahapatra, DA, "TAPI is a Peace Pipeline", part of Russia& India report, 20 Nov 2012

Money Control.com, "ONGC Signs MoU for Mangalore LNG Terminal, dated 20 Mar 2013, uploaded on www.moneycontrol.com/news/ business/ongc-signs-mou-for-mangalore-lng-terminal_840392.html

Nidhi Verma & Jo Winterbottom, "GAIL targets Bigger Presencein Global LNG Trading", reported by Reuters 15 Apr2013, uploaded on in.reuters.com/article/2013/04/15/india-gail-lng-trading-id/ NDEE93EOAT20130415

Oil Industry Development Board, " National gas hydrate Programme", uploaded on oidb.gov.in/index3.asp?sslid=257&sublinkid=69 retrieved on 04 May 2013

Pakistan News service, "Bangladesh Decides to join TAPI Gas Pipeline Project", Pak Tribune dated 07 June 2012.

Parliament proceedings: Reply of Smt Panbakka Lakshmi, Minister of State of Petroleum and Natural Gas to a question by Sri Anto Anthony in Lok Sabha on 22 Feb 2013.

"Project.Focus: Iran-Pak-India Gas Pipeline", pub in Gulf Oil Gas Com Grow, uploaded on www.gulfoilandgas.com/webpro1/ projects/3dreport.aspid=100730

Press Trust of India, "Oil Pipeline to Wagah on the Cards: Report," The Financial Express, May 30, 2012.

Quote from Turkmen minister of Economy and Development Babaamyarat Tuganov at World Economic Forum. He confirmed that Turkmenistan has recently diversified export of Gas to China and Iran, "Minister: Turkmenistan Works on Further Diversification of Energy Sources", Published in TREND International News Agency, Azerbaijan, Baku, date line 08 Apr 2013.

Planning commission Government of India,n-1.

Shabbir H Kazmi, " Pakistani Terrorists Blowing up gas pipeline- Op Ed", published in Euroasia Review in Apr 2011 Issue.

R.V. Shahi, Secretary to the Government of India, Ministry of Power, "India's Strategy Toward Energy Development And Energy Security"

Shine Jacob, " Cairn India strikes Oil in Rajasthan, stock Up", Business standard, 18 Apr 2013, uploaded on http://www.business-standard. com/article/companies/cairn-india-strikes-oil-in-rajasthan-stock- up-113040900073_1.html

Shuchi Srivastava, "ONGC Set to Find More Oil Reserves in Mumbai High", pub in Economic Times, dated 15 Apr 2013.

Sunjoy Joshi, "Drilling Deep for Success", published in The Times of India, New Delhi, 04 May 2013

Sun-Joo Ahn and Dagmar Graczyk, "Understanding Energy Challenges in India: Policies, Players and Issues", published in 2012 as part of Partner Country Series of International Energy Agency, uploaded on www.iea.org retrieved in Mar 2012

Svante E. Cornell, "Eurasia Crisis and Opportunity," The Journal of International Security Affairs 11, Fall 2006

"The Iran –Pakistan-India Pipeline Project: Cross Border Gas Pipeline Challenges, A case Study Prepared for the International Gas Union's Gas Market Integration Task Force" uploaded on www.iapg.org.ar/ wgc09/admin/.../iran%20pakistan%india.pdf

"Tapping into Pakistan's Massive Oil and Gas Reserves", uploaded on http://oilprice.com/Energy/crude-oil/Tapping-into-Pakistan's- Massive-Oil-and-Gas-Reserves.html, retrieved on 18 Jan 2013

Tridivesh Singh Maini and Manish Vaid, "Roadblocks remain to TAPI Pipeline Construction", pub in Oil & Gas Journal dated 03 apr 2013, uploaded on http://www.ogj.com/index.html

US Energy Information Administration (EIA), "India-Analysis", dated 18 mar 2013, uploaded on www.eia.gov/countries/cab.cfm?figs=IN

USGS, World Conventional Gas Resources, by Basin up loaded on http://

en.wikipedia.org/wiki/Natural_gas_reserves_in_Iran retrieved on 06 May 2013.

Undiscovered Oil and Gas Resources of Lower Silurian Qusaiba-Paleozoic Total Petroleum Systems uploaded on http://en.wikipedia.org/wiki/Natural_gas_reserves_in_Iran retrieved on 06 May 2013

Upstream Online (NHST Media Group)). 2007-02-19. Retrieved 2007-12-23

Vaid, M. "Oil Trade Helps Fuel Peace Engagements," Tehelka Magazine, July 26, 2012.

Vargonda Kesava Chandra,"the pipeline That Wasn't: Myanmar-Bangladesh-India Natural gas Pipeline", pub in Journal of Energy Security dated Apr 2012, retrieved on 19 Apr 2013.

www.en.wikipedia.org/wiki/list_of_lng_terminals

www.ingramcontent.com/pod-product-compliance
Lightning Source LLC
Chambersburg PA
CBHW071233290326
41931CB00037B/2846